25 WALKS

In and Around
LONDON

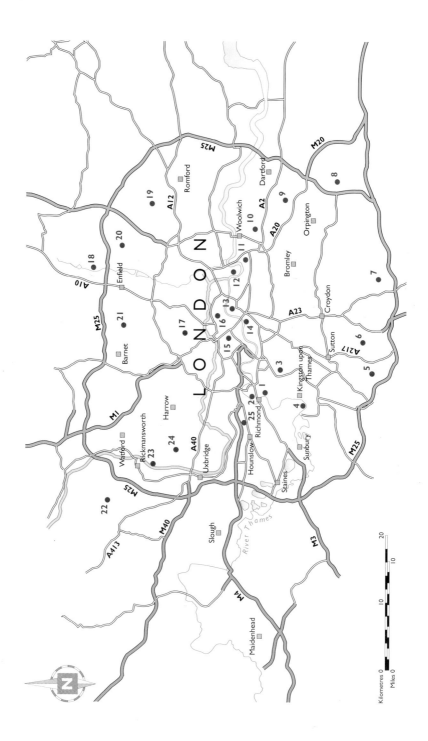

25 WALKS

In and Around

LONDON

Andrew McCloy

Series Editor: Roger Smith

LONDON WALKING FORUM

THE STATIONERY OFFICE

First published 1997

Applications for reproduction should be made to The Stationery Office

Acknowledgements

I am grateful to Simon Kemp and the London Walking Forum for all their help and advice, and to David Sharp for access to his splendid photographs. Thanks also to the Royal Parks, Corporation of London, National Trust, Lee Valley Park and all the officers from the various London boroughs, district and county councils for their assistance. The Woodland Trust and Downlands Countryside Management Project were especially helpful; as were Tom Ridgway at Battersea Park, Denis McGuinnes at Hampton Court Palace and Brian Ancove of United Racecourses. Finally, my gratitude to Katherine and Jenny for contributing in their own special way to a capital project.

British Library Cataloguing in Publication Data

A catalogue record for this book is available from the British Library

ISBN 0 11 495797 5

CONTENTS

USEFUL INFORMATION

For general enquiries contact the following tourist information centres:

Bexley: Central Library, Townley Road, Bexleyheath DA6 7HJ, tel 0181 303 9052.

Croydon: Katharine Street, Croydon CR9 1ET, tel 0181 253 1009.

Greenwich: 46 Greenwich Church Street, London SE10 9BL, tel 0181 858 6376.

Hackney: Central Hall, Mare Street, London E8 1HE, tel 0181 985 9055.

Harrow: Civic Centre, Station Road, Harrow HA1 2XF, tel 0181 424 1100.

Hillingdon: Central Library, 14 High Street, Uxbridge UB8 1HD, tel 01895 250706.

Hounslow: 24 The Treaty Centre, High Street, Hounslow TW3 1ES, tel 0181 572 8279.

Islington: 44 Duncan Street, London N1 8BW, tel 0171 278 8787.

Kingston: Market House, Market Place, Kingston-upon-Thames KT1 1JS, tel 0181 547 5592.

Lewisham: The Library, 199-201 High Street, London SE13 6LG, tel 0181 297 8317.

Richmond: Old Town Hall, Whittaker Avenue, Richmond-upon-Thames TW9 1TP, tel 0181 940 9125.

Southwark: Lower Level, Cotton's Centre, Middle Yard, London SE1 2QJ, tel 0171 403 8299.

Tower Hamlets: 107a Commercial Street, London E1 6BG, tel 0171 375 2549.

Twickenham: 44 York Street, Twckenham TW1 3BZ, tel 0181 891 1411

Other centres are located at Heathrow Airport, Liverpool Street Underground Station, Selfridges (Basement Services Arcade), Waterloo International, Victoria Station and the British Travel Centre (12 Regent Street, Piccadilly Circus). Further details on visiting the City are available from the City of London Information Bureau, St Paul's Churchyard, London EC4M 8BX, tel 0171 606 3030.

Other useful addresses

London Walking Forum, Myddelton House, Bull's Cross, Enfield EN2 9HG (enclose SAE).

Pedestrians' Association, 126 Aldersgate Street, London EC1A 4JQ, tel 0171 490 0750.

Ramblers' Association, 1-5 Wandsworth Road, London SW8 2XX, tel 0171 582 6878.

Woodland Trust, Autumn Park, Dysart Road, Grantham NG31 6LL, tel 01476 581111.

Public Transport

For details of London buses and Underground, call London Transport Travel Information on 0171 222 1234; or the recorded 24-hour Travelcheck on 0171 222 1200. A free tube map is available from any underground station, and for a copy of the excellent 'All London Bus Guide' (also free) and local timetables enquire at your nearest bus garage or travel information centre; or call 0171 371 0247. For enquiries about rail services contact the relevant railway station or consult local directories.

METRIC MEASUREMENTS

At the beginning of each walk, the distance is given in miles and kilometres. Within the text, all measurements are metric for simplicity (and indeed our Ordnance Survey maps are now all metric). However, it was felt that a conversion table might be useful to those readers who still tend to think in Imperial terms.

The basic statistic to remember is that one kilometre is five-eighths of a mile. Half a mile is equivalent to 800 metres and a quarter-mile is 400 metres. Below that distance, yards and metres are little different in practical terms.

km	miles
1	0.625
1.6	1
2	1.25
3	1.875
3.2	2
4	2.5
4.8	3
5	3.125
6	3.75
6.4	4
7	4.375
8	5
9	5.625
10	6.25
16	10

INTRODUCTION

It is tempting to assume that there is not much for the walker in a large capital city such as London, apart from a few well-known parks and the odd bit of riverside. But did you know that there are a staggering 1,700 parks and open spaces throughout Greater London? And that the recently-launched Thames Path, which runs for 288 km (180 miles) from the Barrier to its Gloucestershire source, allows you to walk often traffic-free along nearly all of the capital's riverbank upstream from Docklands? And that's just the start. Above all else, London and its environs offers the enterprising rambler tremendous variety. The 25 walks that follow include heaths and commons, rivers and canals, woodland and downland, royal parks and country parks. From ancient forest to landscaped gardens; Regency terraces to the post-modern shapes of today's Docklands. Choose between the bustling royal Thames and the unhurried Grand Union Canal; the racehorses training on Epsom Downs and the kite-fliers in action on Blackheath or Hampstead Heath. Discover the pines and wood ants of Joyden's Wood, or the ancient oaks and hornbeams of Epping and Hainault Forests.

Best of all, there are a growing number of walking routes for you to explore. Parks and open spaces apart, the following 25 short walks introduce you to some of the most delectable of London's established trails: the Thames Path (Walks 1, 2, 4, 11, 12, 13, 14) and the Grand Union Canal Walk (16, 23, 25); to the south the Banstead and Woldingham Countryside Walks (6, 7), Darent Valley Path (8), Cray Riverway (9) and the Green Chain Walk (10). Across the Thames are the Lea Valley Walk (18), Three Forests Way (19, 20) and the Chess Valley Walk (22), while in the west are the Hillingdon Trail (23, 24) and Brent River Park Walk (25).

All you need is a one-day travelcard and a little enterprise. Take friends or the family, and make sure to pack a picnic. Also, don't forget to be inquisitive. There are walks in this book that explore not just the history of a city but the history of a country. Then there are others on the periphery of the metropolis where a day out becomes a highly enjoyable natural history lesson. Woldingham, Darent Valley, Epping Forest, Chess Valley are well under an hour's tube or train ride from central London and yet deep in the countryside. You will even find that it is possible to walk in central London (South Bank, Regent's Canal, Royal Parks) and explore the capital's heritage but largely avoid a constant barrage of traffic.

Since 1990 walking in the capital has been promoted by the London Walking Forum, a partnership of official bodies and recreational groups such as the Countryside Commission, Sports Council, London Planning Advisory Committee, Lee Valley Park Authority, Ramblers' Association and all the

London Boroughs. Its aim is to create a 2,000 km (1,250-mile) 'Walkers Web', a network of walking routes throughout Greater London, all of it linking to the public transport system. The Forum encourages high standards of information, waymarking and all-round access, and awards its coveted seal of approval to those walks which fulfil its criteria. Most are featured, at least in part, in the routes in this book, and are identified in the text. Others include the Sutton Countryside Walk and River Crane Walk (in West London). There are two longer, more ambitious trails that the Forum is directly involved in developing: the London LOOP (London Outer Orbital Path) and the Capital RING. At 240 km (150 miles) the LOOP will encircle London, and several of its 24 stages have already been opened; while the 115 km (72-mile) RING will provide an inner orbital route for Londoners on foot. Before long the walker's M25 and North/South Circular will be a reality - but without the tarmac and the traffic! For further details contact the London Walking Forum at the address in the Useful Information section.

All 25 walks in this book are accessible by public transport, and you are strongly urged to use it. Almost half are suitable for pushchairs/wheelchairs (the odd bit of heavy ground after rain notwithstanding), and these are indicated in the information panels - which also have details about what footwear is advisable.

Finally, do take care at any road crossing, especially if your companions are very young. London's impatient traffic doesn't always know when to stop. But if you take a train, tube or bus and use your feet to discover this dynamic and fascinating city, at least there will be one less vehicle about. According to official figures, the average speed of motorised vehicles within the M25 is 10 mph, and in central London it is just 6 mph. Why, you find yourself wondering, don't more drivers try walking instead?

ANDREW McCLOY

Opposite: A view of the City from Hampstead Heath.

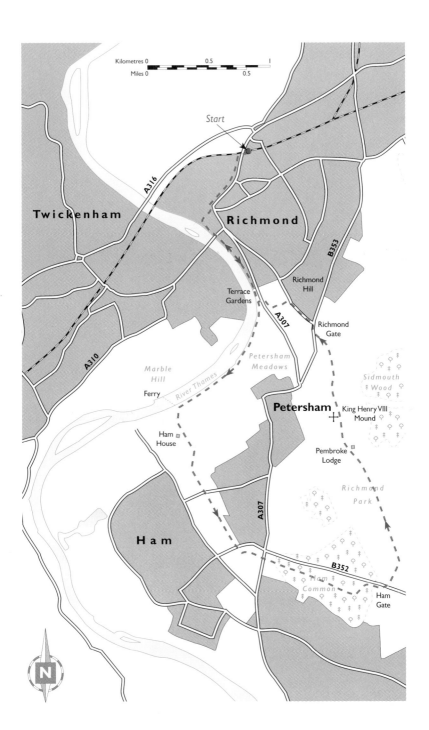

RICHMOND

This is a walk fit for a king! Alongside the most regal of rivers, past an elegant stately house, through an historic royal deer park, and back to a bustling riverside town that has never been out of fashion since the Tudor monarchs first came to stay.

Cross the road outside the station and head left along the busy high street. Turn right down Whittaker Street via the museum and tourist information centre for Richmond's stylish new river terrace, designed by architect Quinlan Terry. On a sunny afternoon the imposing series of neo-Georgian facades look down on promenaders and picnickers by the hundred, and it is a splendid place from which to start your royal ramble.

Follow the Thames Path upstream under the 18th century road bridge. The hubbub quickly subsides, with the geese and cattle of Petersham Meadows providing a more peaceful scene. (If this part of the towpath is flooded, take alternative public footpaths across the Meadows via Petersham.) Soon after the trees close in leave the riverbank opposite Hammerton's foot ferry - a notice says 'Ferry running. Adults 40p, children 20p. Please shout' - and follow a short path through a gateway to reach the imposing frontage of Ham House.

INFORMATION

Distance: 9.5 km (6 miles)

Start and finish: Richmond Station

Terrain: Surfaced and parkland tracks, the latter rough and slippery after rain, when stout footwear is advisable. Note: dogs must be kept under close control in the vicinity of the Park's deer.

Public transport: Richmond Station (trains from Waterloo and District Line tube, plus North London Line); buses 33, 90, 190, 290, 337, 391, H37, R61, R68, R70

Refreshments: Wide choice of pubs and cafes in Richmond town centre and riverfront; plus the Orangery tearoom at Ham House, and Pembroke Lodge in Richmond Park

Opening hours: Richmond Park opens 0700 (summer) and 0730 (winter), and closes at dusk; Ham House, 30 Mar-30 Oct, Mon-Wed 1300-1700, Sat/Sun 1200-1730 (admission charge) but garden open all year (free).

Ham House.

Built about 1610 by Sir Thomas Vavasour, Knight Marshall to King James I, its manicured gardens and lavish Stuart interior are extremely well preserved. Now managed by the National Trust, it is open to the public.

Follow the wide, divided track around the outer wall of Ham House; then at the far end veer half-right on to a path across rough ground to join a long bridleway, with Ham House now visible behind. Cross a road and continue to the wide green at Ham, a very villagey sort of place. Go left, away from the pond, and across the busy A307 which is safely negotiated via a pedestrian crossing (there is also a crossing for our equestrian friends, with a flashing red/green horse symbol). On the far side follow the wood-chipped horse ride or any of the complementary small tracks for 800 m across Ham Common to Ham Gate, and enter Richmond Park.

The park is one of those priceless green lungs that makes living in the big smoke bearable. It was a popular royal hunting ground from Tudor times. Charles I (taking his court to Richmond to escape the plague) enclosed the parkland with a 13 km wall, but in 1751 local people broke back in and re-established public access. Although still a Royal Park, its 1,000 hectares contain a wide variety of habitats, from acidic grassland to bogs and stands of ancient oak. Some of the present-day oaks predate the original enclosure, and are home to owls, rare beetles and bats. Britain's largest bat, the noctule, thrives in the dry old oaks and ash holes of the park when elsewhere in London it is declining.

But for many people the park is best-known for its herds of red and fallow deer, almost 700 of which roam here. The red deer is Britain's largest land mammal, with a reddish-brown coat which turns grey-brown in winter. Stags have narrow, many-pointed antlers which are shed each March, and they are named according to how many points they possess. A stag with six on each antler is known as a 'Royal', and a mighty seven makes him an 'Imperial'. Fallow deer are smaller, with a dappled summer coat of distinctive white spots.

Do remember that the deer in Richmond Park are essentially wild, so don't try to feed them or get too close, especially when the calves (red deer) and fawns (fallow) are born in May or June, at which times the mothers are understandably protective; and also when the stags rut in October. Periodically, Royal Park officials act to control deer numbers, but they have to get Her Majesty's signature first. The Royal Venison Warrant is still needed to cull the animals, dating back to the time when equal sanctity was attached to men and deer alike.

From Ham Gate, go past the pond and head diagonally left to the ridge that rises above the long green strip of Petersham Park. A broad track known as Hornbeam Walk runs along the top, and as you follow this northwards the trees thin out and the views improve. At this point the energetic may like to consider a brief excursion into the middle of the park to enjoy the Isabella Plantation - the azaleas and rhododendrons are particularly colourful in May and June.

View from Richmond Hill.

Enter the gate of Pembroke Lodge, which Queen Victoria gave to her Prime Minister Lord John Russell in 1846, and which was later the boyhood home of his grandson, the philosopher Bertrand Russell. It is now a popular and well-stocked tearoom. Further on are colourful flower beds, and King Henry VIII Mound.

His Majesty used to observe the hunts from here, and legend has it that this was also where he stood awaiting sight of a rocket signalling Anne Boleyn's execution at the Tower. Today the panorama westwards include Heathrow, Twickenham rugby stadium and Windsor Castle, while in the hedge behind you is the 'keyhole', a narrow cutting through which you have an amazingly uninterrupted view of St Paul's Cathedral, 10 miles/16 km away in the City of London (weather permitting!).

Richmond waterfront.

Go through the unwieldy, deer-proof Lodge gate, and on to Richmond Gate. When leaving the park be careful of traffic at the busy junction - it's best to use the two zebra crossings to reach the pavement of Richmond Hill in front of the Star and Garter Home for ex-servicemen. Soon you come to the Terrace Walk, a wide gravel walkway with famous views down to the tree-lined river. Save some camera film for this spot!

From here take a steep, surfaced path down into and through the Terrace Gardens, where the ornamental collection includes a tulip tree and strawberry tree. Above the lower lawn lounges the Coadestone River God statue. To return to the riverside and Richmond town centre, leave the park by a tiny pedestrian subway under the road (it is locked when the gates of the garden are secured, usually around early evening).

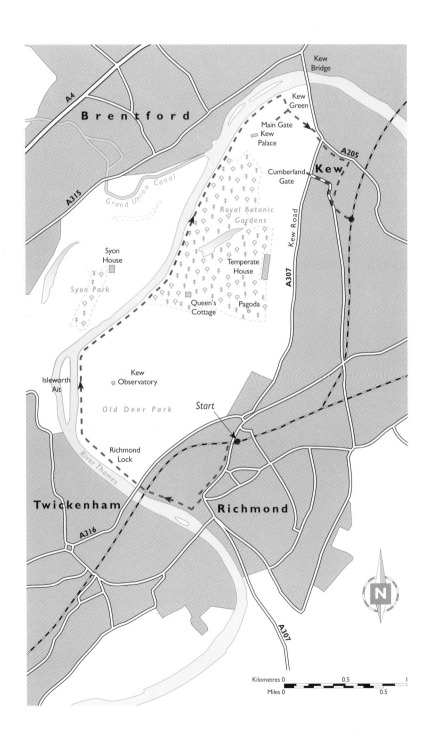

KEW GARDENS

Like the Natural History Museum or the Victoria & Albert Museum, the Royal Botanic Gardens at Kew is one of those places where there is simply not enough time to appreciate everything in one visit. It's a place that fascinates adults and children alike, whether you enjoy a 3,500 million-year history lesson at Evolution House, a quiet stroll through the tranquil woodlands by the river, or a sweaty tour of the Palm House or Waterlily House amid gigantic rainforest plants. And what better way of preparing for it than by a stroll along a particularly quiet and leafy stretch of the Thames?

For town centre directions through Richmond, see Walk 1. At the river, turn right and follow the wide towpath downstream past the White Cross Hotel and underneath the railway and road crossings. Ahead is Richmond Lock (a lock and weir, really), with its unusual overhead footbridge to the Middlesex shore. After the Thames Barrier, this is only the second tidal control on the Thames upstream.

The wide and gentle towpath between Richmond and Kew is a popular section of the Thames Path, and walkers should beware occasional speeding cyclists - even though a byelaw technically prohibits cycling along the pathway. The further towards Kew, the more rewarding the journey becomes: trees and parkland clothe either side and only the throaty roar of a jet making its noisy final approach to Heathrow reminds you that Marble Arch and the West End are little more than 10 km away.

In midstream is the long, wooded screen of Isleworth Ait (ait is a term for an island in a river, often associated with the Thames), a popular spot for nesting herons. This is finally replaced by Syon Park on the far bank, and at the water's edge there is an unusual tide meadow, where the river creeps into inlet channels twice a day to flood the shore. The broad, rectangular mansion of Syon House is still owned by the

INFORMATION

Distance: 6.5 km (4 miles).

Start: Richmond Station.

Finish: Kew Gardens Station.

Terrain: Easy towpath; no special footwear necessary. Accessible for pushchairs/wheelchairs

Public transport: Both stations are on the District Line tube (only a three-minute ride apart), and Richmond also connects with Waterloo and the North London Line; for buses see Walk 1, from Kew 65, 391, R68 (Sun only).

Refreshments: Plenty of cafes and pubs in centre of Richmond and Kew Gardens; plus cafes/restaurants in Botanic Gardens.

Opening hours: Royal Botanic Gardens, daily, 0930-1630/1730, park until dusk (admission charge).

Further reading: Thames Path National Trail Guide by David Sharp (Aurum Press, 1996).

Top: Thames Path, opposite Isleworth.

Bottom: Thames Path, near Syon House.

Northumberland family, whose leaping stone lion adorns the roof.

To your right, across the overflow ditch, is the huge green expanse of the Old Deer Park, including a recreation ground and golf course. The Observatory in its centre was built by command of George III. Soon the Royal Botanic Gardens begin, and here in the unspoilt western corner (the 'conservation area') the rich canopy ranges from oak and birch to giant red-woods. In between are the Bamboo Garden, Rhododendron Dell, and much more besides. It is tempting to enter by the Brentford Gate nearby, but wait a little longer if you can!

The opposite bank becomes rather more built-up now, and here the Grand Union Canal meets the Thames, after its 240 km journey from the centre of Birmingham (although today many canal-users take the eastern branch through London to Little Venice and Paddington). In winter cormorants can be seen roosting in the tall trees of Brentford Ait.

With Kew Bridge virtually in sight, leave the riverside by turning right, down Ferry Lane. This brings you on to the wide, neat green at Kew, where the tree-lined cricket pitch is overlooked by respectable Georgian town houses. The main entrance of the Gardens is over to your right.

A botanic garden was first begun in earnest on this site by Princess Augusta in 1759, and continued by her son, George III. It soon became a major centre of botanical research. Captain Cook and Charles Darwin always returned from their voyages with new specimens for the collection at Kew, and from here quinine was first taken to India in 1860, and rubber trees introduced to Malaysia in 1875. Today you can marvel at an array of rainforest species in the gigantic Palm House; or at the collection of Mediterranean plants in the Temperate House.

Equally awe-inspiring is the new Princess of Wales Conservatory, a remarkable construction in which you can walk through ten computer-controlled climatic zones. In addition, the 120 ha site includes numerous lakes and ornamental flower beds, a waterfowl collection, a gallery of botanical painting, plus the famous 50 m-high pagoda which Sir William Chambers designed for Princess Augusta in 1761 when the 'Chinese style' was the in thing.

There is also Kew Palace, one of the smallest of the former royal residences, where George III and Queen Charlotte lived for some years. It was near here, by the river, that His Majesty lived out the last, sad years of his life insane. Today, Kew Gardens remains a top visitor attraction, but it also continues to fulfil its role as one of the world's leading centres of botanical record and research, and it is currently developing an internationally important seedbank.

To reach the tube station from the Gardens, leave by Cumberland Gate and cross Kew Road to take Kew Gardens Road opposite, which leads to Station Approach; otherwise follow the path over the green past the Parish Church of St Anne, where the painter Thomas Gainsborough is buried, and cross Kew Road at the lights. Walk down Mortlake Road to Leybourne Road, and either this or Atwoods Alley will deliver you to Station Approach.

Thames Path, near Kew.

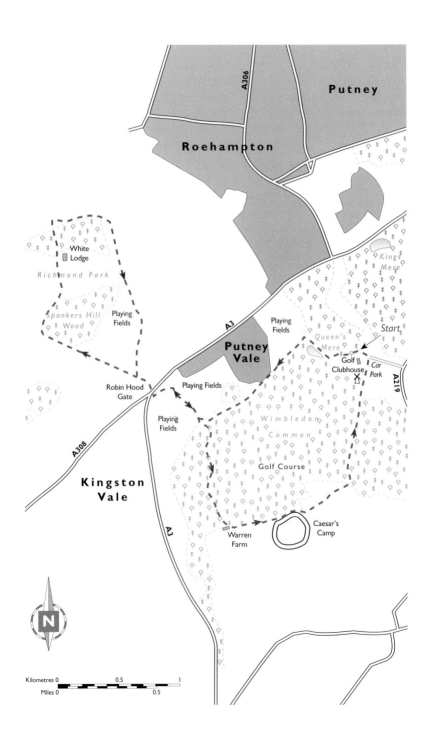

WIMBLEDON COMMON

SW19's sprawling common is nowadays London's largest, but it might have vanished long ago had the Lord of the Manors of Wimbledon and Battersea had his way in the 1860s. The long campaign against the Earl of Spencer's planned enclosure eventually resulted in the Wimbledon and Putney Commons Act of 1871, and since then the commons have been carefully managed by a small group of local representatives known as the Conservators.

Over the years Wimbledon Common has been used for some curious activities. Duels were often fought here, one involving Prime Minister William Pitt and Southwark MP George Tierney after a parliamentary quarrel (neither was hurt - it is assumed that they both deliberately missed). For almost 30 years the National Rifle Association had a large enclosure on the Common, and their inaugural meeting was opened in 1860 by Queen Victoria, who fired the first shot.

Whether you are into windmills or wombles this is splendid walking country, and it begins as soon as you leave the large car park opposite (but not alongside) the clubhouse entrance of the London Scottish Golf Club, from where a well-walked path descends through thick woodland to Queen's Mere, surrounded by its high wall of trees. Each year a pair of coots nest on the artificial pond, while under the surface, common toads spawn after hibernating on dry land for five months.

Follow the right-hand bank and at the far end there is a short, straight track ahead through the wood. Turn left on to the Stag Ride, popular with horses but wide enough to accommodate all users. Through the trees on your right is Putney Vale Cemetery, and a little further on a war memorial is set in the corner of playing fields.

INFORMATION

Distance: 9.5 km (6 miles), or shorter route 5 km (3 miles).

Start and finish: Windmill car park, off A219 (Parkside).

Terrain: Gentle heath and woodland tracks, but some of the latter will be muddy after rain, making stout footwear necessary. Note: In Richmond Park dogs must be kept under close control in the vicinity of deer (and see other comments in Walk 1).

Public transport: Bus 93 at end of Windmill Road, on Parkside.

Refreshments: Windmill cafe; Duke of Cambridge pub (Kingston Vale, off A3).

Opening hours: Wimbledon Windmill Museum, Apr-Oct, Sat, Sun and public holidays, 1400-1700 (admission charge).

Wimbledon Common's famous windmill.

After 1 km of rolling woodland the track comes to a triangular junction. If you don't want to visit Richmond Park carry straight on (the shorter route), otherwise turn right, then 100 m later veer right once more, keeping the brook on your left. Nearing the sports pavilion go over the stone bridge (left), and across an open field for the footbridge over the busy A3. On the other side cross Kingston Vale, opposite the Duke of Cambridge pub, and enter Richmond Park via the Robin Hood Gate.

Now the scenery changes completely. Cross the road beyond the car park for glorious open parkland, making for the left-hand corner of Spankers Hill Wood. Skirting the ancient woodland, follow the direction of the closed-off road northwards to White Lodge. Deer may be quietly watching from the trees, while on your left there are expansive views of the

Pen Ponds in winter.

park, with Pen Ponds glistening in the distance. During World War II these former gravel pits were drained to prevent them becoming a landmark for enemy bombers, but, since restored, they have become home to grebes, pochard, tufted duck and mute swans.

Go past White Lodge, now occupied by the Royal Ballet School, and when the road emerges from the trees, turn off right along a faint grassy track, with the flats of Roehampton ahead. Don't drop down to the road but turn right, back into patchy woodland, and go past the tiny Queen Mother's Copse (the fence keeps the deer out and allows daffodils and bluebells to survive). Keep to the obvious track straight ahead, which soon descends to playing fields below the thick spinney. Cross these and retrace your steps to Wimbledon Common.

Back at the triangular meeting of tracks (the short walk resumes here) turn right, and right again at a fork, and continue along this pleasant, wooded ride all the way to Warren Farm, where the rising track swings left and becomes more gravelly. Oak now gives way to silver birch, and there is more of a heathland feel. Behind the fence on your right is the Royal Wimbledon Golf Course, and straddling the fairway a low bank represents the ramparts of Caesar's Camp - nothing to with the Romans, but an Iron Age hillfort.

Curving right at the top of the hill, take the second path off left (between wooden posts - but not the white ones) and cross two fairways. Do look first to see if any golfers are in action! Cross a small lane near Springwell Cottage and go through a white barrier to join a wide and popular unmade track, known as Inner Windmill Road, back to the start.

For those keen to sample the cafes of Wimbledon village, turn right on to the Memorial Ride, and perhaps return past Bluegate Gravel Pit, now a pretty little pond. Lastly, don't forget to visit the windmill. The last hollow-post flour mill left in England, it was built in 1817 but renovated several times since, and is now an interesting museum showing the history of windmills. In the early 19th century its miller was also required to act as local constable, keeping watch from the top of the mill, not just for local ruffians but also illegal duellists!

Wimbledon Common.

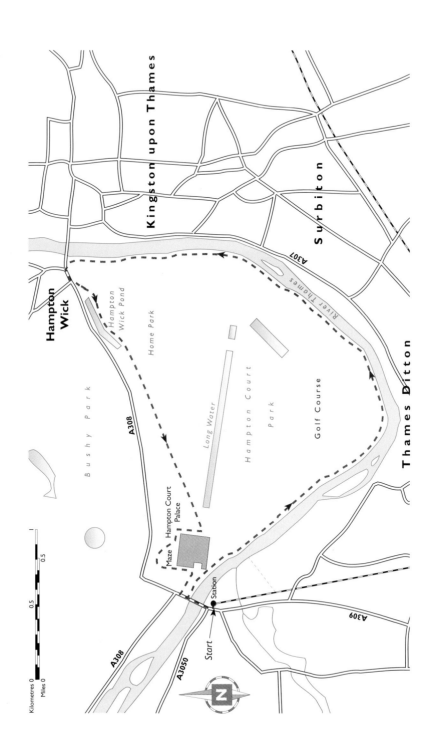

HAMPTON COURT

Over the centuries a variety of royal buildings have sprung up along the banks of the Thames. Some convey a sense of might and power, notably the proud ramparts of Windsor Castle and the sturdy walls of the Tower of London, while others like Kew Palace are genteel and retiring. Several don't even exist any more, such as Whitehall, and the once splendid Shene Palace at Richmond, built by Henry VII on the site of earlier versions, and later one of the homes of his energetic second son. But when Henry VIII tired of Richmond and Greenwich, he looked further upriver to Hampton Court Palace, which to this day remains one of the most attractive and best-preserved royal premises in the London area.

Leave the station and cross the river by the bridge, then turn right to join the Thames Path. The first view of the Palace is of the Tudor red-brick West

Hampton Court Palace.

Front, with its intricate forest of chimneys and towers; but as you begin to move past the building the elegant Baroque facade created by Christopher Wren reveals itself, with the beautiful wrought iron screens made by 17th century French metalsmith Jean Tijou hiding the now restored Privy Garden. You will have a chance to see all this in greater detail later.

Follow the wide towpath, known as the Barge Walk, for four easy kilometres as the river gently loops round to Kingston Bridge (in Old English, Hampton means

INFORMATION

Distance: 8.5 km (5.25 miles).

Start and finish: Hampton Court Station.

Terrain: Easy paths. No special footwear necessary. Accessible for pushchairs/ wheelchairs (but rough grass in Home Park).

Public transport: Hampton Court Station (trains from Waterloo); buses 111, 216, 415, 440, 461, 513, R68, 718, 726.

Refreshments: pubs and cafes by Hampton Court Bridge; Old Kings Head, by Kingston Bridge; Tiltyard Tearooms in Palace grounds.

Opening hours: Mid Mar to mid Oct 0930-1800, mid Oct to mid Mar 0930-1630 (admission charge to Maze, Palace and Privy Garden, other gardens and grounds free).

Note: access is severely restricted during the annual flower show each July, and the East Front gardens are closed each day from 1700 during the Music Festival in June.

'land in the bend of the river'). It is a quiet and surprisingly rural passage, with a welcome absence of roads and houses for some considerable distance. On your left is Hampton Court Park, plus a golf course, and a number of gates along the way offer access.

At Kingston Bridge turn left and almost immediately left again, by the Old Kings Head pub, into Home Park. After 100 m veer right, past Hampton Wick Pond, then ahead to enter a grassy, tree-lined avenue all the way to the palace (the gaps in the rows of mature lime trees are

due to the Great Storm of October 1987). Across the park to your left is the Long Water, which Charles II had dug in 1662; it occupies the middle of three grand avenues that radiate out from the palace. Cross the semi-circular canal to enter the Fountain Garden, with its rows of clipped yews, immaculate lawns and gravel paths.

Long Water, Hampton Court Park.

Hampton Court began as a modest, 12th century manor owned by a holy order, the Knights Hospitallers. In 1514, Henry VIII's all-powerful minister, Cardinal Wolsey, obtained the lease and set about building a grand residence, but in 1528 he gave it up to the King in an attempt to win back his favour (it didn't work, and Wolsey died discredited in 1530). Henry continued the additions, quadrupling the size of the kitchens to feed the royal retinue and completing the impressive Great Hall. Building work largely ceased with the Stuarts, although they continued to use Hampton Court. Charles I had the dubious distinction of staying first as a reigning monarch and then later as a prisoner of Oliver Cromwell during the Civil War.

With the Restoration, William and Mary employed Christopher Wren to redesign the Palace in the contemporary Baroque style, and although George II was the last monarch to live in the Palace it is still owned by the sovereign, and indeed the buildings and grounds remain well-tended, to the extent that in the last few years William III's abandoned Privy Garden has been painstakingly restored to its original 1702 layout. In addition, former servants of the Crown live in apartments at the Palace known as Grace and Favour residences - these too have been restored after a serious fire a few years ago.

Walk around the northern side of the Palace, and here you will find the famous Maze. Planted in the 1690s, it has been bewildering hapless visitors ever since, and for a small charge you too can get completely lost. The Maze is the last surviving part of an area known as the Wilderness, and nearby are the Tiltyard Gardens, which back on to the restaurant and cafeteria.

If the day is still young and you have plenty of energy, leave the grounds via the Lion Gate, beyond the Maze, and cross Hampton Court Road for Bushy Park. Like Richmond Park, it was a former hunting ground for Henry VIII, and still boasts several hundred deer, plus ornamental gardens and ponds. Otherwise, follow the signs past the Wilderness back to the main entrance, where you can either leave via the Trophy Gate for the bridge and railway station, or go in to view the sumptuous interior of the Palace.

Here you can inspect the state apartments of Henry VIII and Queen Mary, the Georgian Rooms, and the Renaissance Gallery which includes paintings from the Royal Collection. You can even see a banquet being prepared in the Tudor kitchen. And they had quite an appetite!

Hampton Wick Pond, Home Park.

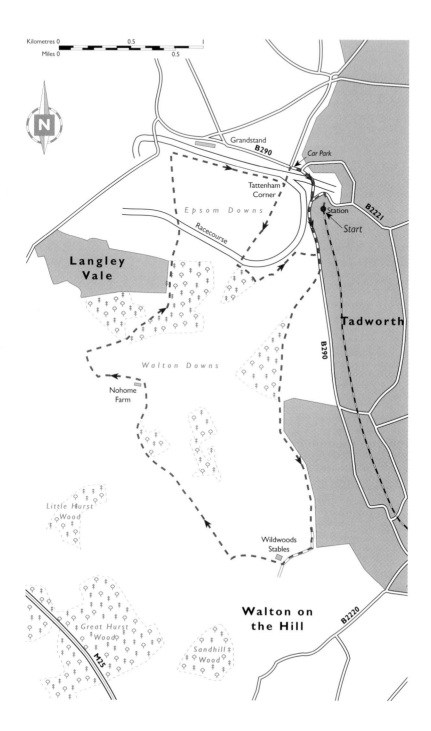

Kilometres 0   0.5   1
Miles 0   0.5

N

Grandstand
B290
Car Park
Tattenham
Corner
Epsom Downs
Racecourse
Station
Start
B2221

**Langley
Vale**

Tadworth

Walton Downs
B290
Nohome
Farm

*Little Hurst
Wood*

Wildwoods
Stables

**Walton on
the Hill**
B2220

*Great Hurst
Wood*
M25

*Sandhill
Wood*

EPSOM DOWNS

For most of the year Epsom Downs is a relatively quiet place, where you can take a stroll on the high, windy turf and admire the views. Not so on the day of the Derby, the famous horse race for three-year-old thoroughbreds held here every June. Altogether there are usually between 8 and 11 days racing each year, occasions when this walk is to be avoided since public access across the downs is temporarily restricted.

For those arriving by car, park at the top of the course, close to The Tattenham Corner pub. Follow the access road across the race track, with the gleaming white grandstands at the bottom of the hill, then take the bridleway ahead of you that cuts across the open downs occupying the middle of the course. On the far side a crowd of model aircraft enthusiasts regularly gather, and the skies are often full of buzzing miniature planes.

Model aircraft on Epsom Downs.

At the 8-furlong post go across the track once more, turn left, then almost immediately right, on a signposted footpath into trees. Keep straight on and before long you emerge at the top of Walton Downs, where each day between 0615 and 1200 racehorses are exercised on marked gallops. It goes without saying that you should keep a safe and respectful distance between these times, and ensure that dogs are under tight control.

INFORMATION

Distance: 8.5 km (5.25 miles).

Start and finish: Tattenham Corner (railway station, or any of the car parks at top of race course).

Terrain: Rough downland and a potentially muddy woodland stretch, so strong footwear is advisable.

Public transport: Tattenham Corner Station (trains from Victoria); buses 406, 727 (Mon-Sat).

Refreshments: The Tattenham Corner (restaurant/pub); The Downs Lunch Box (at car park).

Opening hours: The Derby Day Experience (includes tour of the Queen's Stand, Jockeys' Changing Room, Museum, etc) open on specific dates only (admission charge). Contact The Racecourse, Epsom Downs, Surrey KT18 5LQ, tel 01372 726311.

Note: access and car parking restricted on race days.

Turn left and go past white railings and around the far (eastern) end of the gallops near the road to join the public bridleway at the foot of the slope. *Those who have arrived at Tattenham Corner by train will join here after a 300 m walk along Epsom Lane (B290).* In under 500 m turn left into woodland for a long, straight track that soon runs between the sedate back gardens of Tadworth on one side and ploughed fields on the other.

After 1.5 km you arrive at an unmade lane and turn right. Follow this until about 100 m beyond Wildwoods Stables, then turn right for a footpath that crosses a narrow lane and small field. At the far side turn right onto a long, gently dipping bridleway that offers pleasant views across fields and woodland towards Headley.

In just over 1 km swing left, past the oddly-named Nohome Farm, and continue for 400 m until a footpath branches off uphill to the right between posts. On this small area of hillside widespread coppicing of native hazel is taking place, with the aim of encouraging new shoots (or 'wands') as well as allowing older, untouched trees (known as 'standards') to flourish.

Curving right, join another track to cross Walton Downs once more – and, since it also crosses gallops,

Racehorse gallops on Walton Downs.

look carefully about you first. After 500 m turn left, past a white bar gate, and half-right across a series of wide, grassy clearings amongst woods. Beyond a children's playground enter a thicket in the far corner and turn left on to a wide, well-used track. Follow this past the houses of Langley Vale, across more gallops, then around the edge of bushes, and suddenly the whole of Epsom Downs racecourse is revealed before you.

Squeeze through the narrow gap in the white railings and follow the public footpath across the racetrack (how lush the turf is!). On the far side there is a

The racecourse.

choice of three footpaths across the downs towards the grandstands, although only the left-hand one is well-defined. Now, well away from the model aircraft, you may see skylarks and meadow pipits. In front of the gigantic white grandstands, turn right and follow the unmade track uphill back to the track-crossing at the start of the walk; and continue a little further along the edge of the main road to reach the station. If you want to visit the Queen's Stand for the Derby Day Experience (check opening dates in advance), take the foot tunnel under the course.

On Derby Day the normally empty centre of the course is packed with open-top buses, marquees, funfairs and the like; and in case you're wondering, that isolated metal gantry is used to show the numbers of the winning horses and starting prices. As far back as 1683, Charles II came to watch the horses race on Epsom Downs, but it was over a century later that the 12th Earl of Derby established the two now famous races here.

The Oaks, named after his house in Carshalton, was first run in 1779, and a year later the Derby followed. So massively popular did the sporting event become that at one time Parliament used to break off for the whole of Derby week, and in 1921 an airship and the RAF had to be called in to sort out local traffic congestion. The excitement and razzmatazz surrounding the Derby continues, but it is odd to think that the actual event that everyone comes to see is over in less than two minutes.

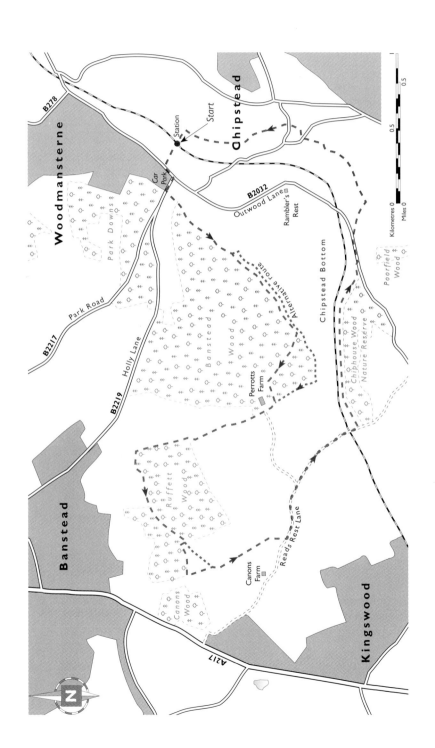

CHIPSTEAD VALLEY

The narrow zone that lies between the southern edge of Greater London and the M25 has something of an identity problem. The leafy drives of Sutton and Croydon come to an end but Surrey doesn't really seem to get going until the North Downs. And yet here, tucked quietly away, are some exquisite pockets of countryside, and none more so than Banstead Woods and Chipstead Valley. The former is a 110 ha mixed wood which sits high above a deep and winding valley chequered with fields and copses, including a Woodland Trust nature reserve, and very much fulfilling Surrey's boast to be the most heavily wooded county in England. Time to explore.

Walk down Station Parade and go left into Outwood Lane. After 100 m cross over and go through a gate to reach Holly Lane car park. The clear path behind the toilet block climbs towards the woods. Go right, through a kissing gate (signposted Banstead Woods Nature Trail), and up a wide, gravelly track that soon levels out. Ignore all tempting paths off to the right; but instead carry on through ancient woodland containing mature oak, sweet chestnut, yew and beech.

Recorded as long ago as the Domesday Book, Banstead Woods were important for the production of compass timber, naturally curved pieces of oak that were vital in the construction of wooden sailing ships. Today the mixed woodland is rich in wildlife, home to all three resident British woodpeckers and in spring is carpeted with primroses, bluebells and wood anemones. There may also be an occasional glimpse of the secretive roe deer, the smaller of Britain's two native deer (the other is the red deer - see Walk 1).

After 2 km the main track eventually bends right, by Nature Trail post No 12, and here turn left, for a short grassy path to Perrotts Farm. Alternatively, if you prefer the butterflies and orchids of the field, there are a series of exits (left) along the woodland ride where

INFORMATION

Distance: 9 km (5.5 miles).

Start and finish: Chipstead Station or Holly Lane car park.

Terrain: Hilly woodland and valley tracks. Strong footwear advisable. Some of the walk follows waymarks for the Banstead Countryside Walk (which has gained the London Walking Forum's seal of approval).

Public transport: Chipstead Station (trains from Victoria); buses 166 and 498 (Mon-Sat).

Refreshments: Ramblers Rest Pub, Outwood Lane (1 km off route); Holly Lane car park kiosk open occasional summer weekends.

Further information: Downlands Countryside Management Project (address and other details in Walk 7).

D.C.M.P.

you can slip through and join the Banstead Countryside Walk beside open meadow and scrub above the valley, eventually turning right, along the woodland edge to Perrotts Farm. Simply follow the waymarks; and if you are very lucky you may even see a sparrowhawk (depicted on the walk's logo), a small but speedy bird of prey often found in forested areas.

At Perrotts Farm, take the bridleway through a gate signposted Holly Lane. This leads gently downhill between fields, and after skirting Ruffett Wood go over a stile and turn left (signposted Burgh Heath). Now, keeping the private woodland on your left, carry straight on along the field edge, then over stiles, past more fields and copses, until a path cuts diagonally left across a field - there is also a public right of way around its right-hand edge if the going is too heavy. At the far side turn left (signposted Reads Rest Lane), along the field edge as far as farm buildings, where you should turn left again into an unmade lane.

Left: Looking across Chipstead valley to Banstead Woods.

Right: Coal Post.

Soon there are eye-catching views over Chipstead Valley, into which you now descend by taking the sunken, resurfaced bridleway that forks half-right through a metal gate (signposted Outwood Lane).

Go under the railway bridge and turn left, into the Woodland Trust's Chiphouse Wood nature reserve. By the gate is a white 'coal post', where between 1666 and 1890 tax was levied on, amongst other things, all coal entering the capital, a measure initially introduced to help finance the rebuilding of the city after the Great Fire of London.

Down in the cool valley bottom all is quiet and peaceful, except when the occasional train clatters along the branch line to Tattenham Corner and back. Oak, ash and beech provide shade, plus there are new areas of broadleaved planting. When the Banstead Countryside Walk turns off, under another bridge, you should continue straight on to Outwood Lane and turn left. If you are in need of refreshment a short pavement walk will bring you to the aptly-named Ramblers Rest, occupying what was until recently the site of the 13th century Dene Farm.

A welcome sign.

Otherwise cross the road after 230 m and take the left of two (somewhat undefined) footpaths diagonally across a broad, sloping field - keep just to the left of two mature trees in the middle of the pasture. At the top go through a gate and over another field to cross a narrow lane. Beware! Castle Road is one-way (downhill only) but the footpath emerges almost blind, so listen first and cross warily.

The clear path continues through thickets, and there are new and stunning views of the valley and woodland fringe from this high eastern rim. Make sure that where the path swings right, deeper into the trees, you keep left, so that the valley bottom is in sight; then after crossing a small field and another road - where the path's hidden entrance again requires care - take a short public footpath into Farm Close and then cross a further lane into Walpole Avenue. At the end of this cul de sac, continue along an alleyway, then left, down steps, to return to the station.

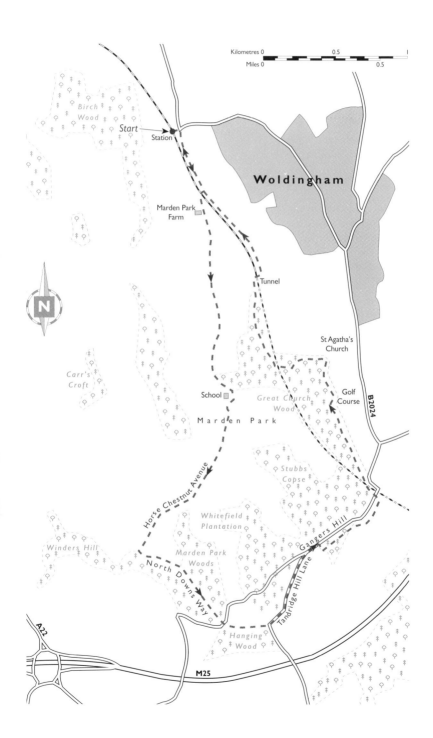

Kilometres 0   0.5   1
Miles 0   0.5

Birch Wood

Start
Station

Woldingham

Marden Park Farm

Tunnel

N

St Agatha's Church

Carr's Croft

School

Golf Course

B2024

Great Church Wood

M a r d e n   P a r k

Stubbs Copse

Horse Chestnut Avenue

Whitefield Plantation

Winders Hill

Marden Park Woods

North Downs Way

Gangers Hill

Tandridge Hill Lane

A22

Hanging Wood

M25

WOLDINGHAM

The Woldingham Countryside Walk, which this walk mostly follows, has gained the London Walking Forum's seal of approval for its all-round high standards. It is one of four excellent circular routes (and two nature trails) created by the Downlands Countryside Management Project - you will have met another near Banstead on Walk 6.

The Project is a partnership of various local authorities, including the London Boroughs of Sutton and Croydon, and the Corporation of London, and aims to promote public access in tandem with careful landscape conservation. Since the Project was started in 1988 over 40 ponds have been restored, 13,000 trees planted and 140 km of rights of way signposted or improved. More details, including leaflet guides for all the routes, are available from the address in the information panel.

At the entrance to Woldingham Station car park, turn right along Church Road and, although it's not actually part of the waymarked walk, turn right over the bridge for a bridleway past Marden Park Farm. There are lovely views over the rolling fields of this peaceful valley; and after the waymarked route enters from the left, drop down to pass the buildings of Woldingham School, a Catholic boarding school for girls. The gothic-looking building was part of the original Marden Park, the village having disappeared long ago in the Black Death. At the turn of the 19th century the park was home to William Wilberforce during his campaign to abolish slavery.

Walk along Horse Chestnut Avenue - some mature specimens do still survive - and at the end is South Lodge, where you should turn left on to the North Downs Way. There is a short, steep climb, allowing expansive views towards Godstone and over the Weald. The path soon levels out and wanders through the beeches and bluebells of Marden Park Woods, where a friendly Woodland Trust sign says 'Visitors are

INFORMATION

Distance: 10.5 km (6.5 miles).

Start and finish: Woldingham Station.

Terrain: Downland and woodland paths, with a couple of steep slopes and steps. Strong footwear advisable. Mainly follows waymarks for the Woldingham Countryside Walk.

Public transport: Woldingham Station (trains from Victoria).

Refreshments: None on route.

Further information: Downlands Countryside Management Project, Highway House, 21 Chessington Road, West Ewell, Epsom, Surrey KT17 1TT, tel 0181 541 7282.

D.C.M.P.

welcome to walk in our woods'. Go across one lane and descend a track to another (Tandridge Hill Lane). Turn left and follow a shaded path next to the road as it climbs uphill. The M25 continues to growl at the foot of the downs, but it will not be your companion for much longer.

Above: Walking through Marden Park Wood.

Below: St Agatha's Church.

At the minor road junction at the top turn right along Gangers Hill, being careful of occasional oncoming traffic, and after 50 m the North Downs Way returns to a hillside track below the road. Around you now is untidy scrubland, with a few stripped, dead trees evident. Little more than a decade ago this hilltop was richly wooded, until in the course of one October night in 1987 hurricane-force winds swept through the South of England, and over 15 million trees were uprooted or damaged.

The North Downs of Surrey and Kent were particularly badly affected, and whole skylines were completely altered within the space of a few hours. But, as is usually the case with Nature, good comes out of destruction, and the huge amounts of decaying wood provided new habitats for various insects, like longhorn beetles whose larvae develop in rotting trees and stumps. This in turn meant more food for birds like woodpeckers and nuthatches; while more moths, gnats and other flying insects meant more food for bats; and so on.

Just before the path turns sharply right, downhill, you turn left and go up a short flight of wooden steps to cross the road for the car park opposite. Through a gate, the Countryside Walk continues along the wide track ahead; after passing some attractive meadowland, take the signposted path up steps to the right through Great Church Wood. Once owned by the conductor Sir Adrian Boult, who lived at nearby South Hawke, the delightful mix of oak, beech and yew is awash with bluebells in the spring (it is now safely in the hands of the Woodland Trust). A short detour is recommended to visit the tiny St Agatha's Church, one of the highest in Surrey (236 m), which is just off the path next to the golf course.

Return downhill to the main track and turn right. Follow it for 150 m until a narrow path branches off to the right, signposted Woldingham Station. This descends through cool, deep woodland, where it is rewarding to stop for a moment and listen to the birdlife. You may hear wood warblers calling "dee-you", or trilling an accelerating series of "sip" notes; and the black-bibbed yellow-breasted great tit singing "teacher, teacher". Blackbirds announce their presence by shuffling noisily about in the undergrowth, while in the treetops there will be woodpigeons clattering or cooing. Perhaps there will even be the occasional hammering of a woodpecker.

At the bottom of the track you pass above the opening of the railway tunnel, built between 1878 and 1884, which has taken the commuters of Surrey and Kent into central London ever since. Go over stiles and turn left into Church Road to return to the station.

View over Woldingham.

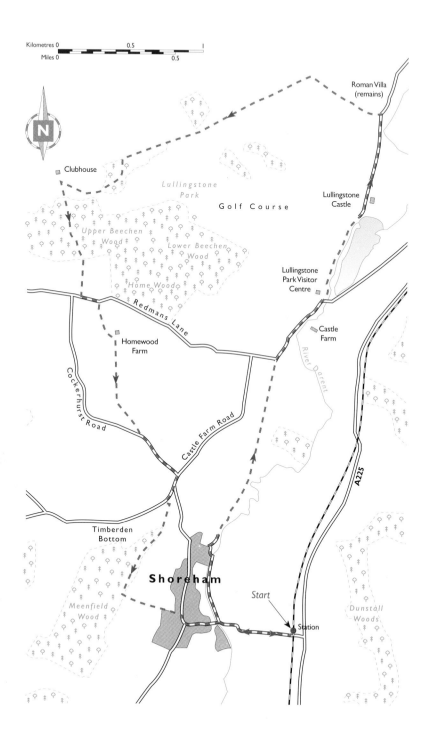

Kilometres 0   0.5   1
Miles 0   0.5

N

Roman Villa
(remains)

Clubhouse

Lullingstone
Park

Golf Course

Lullingstone
Castle

Upper Beechen
Wood

Lower Beechen
Wood

Home Wood

Lullingstone
Park Visitor
Centre

Redmans Lane

Castle
Farm

Homewood
Farm

River Darent

Cockerhurst Road

Castle Farm Road

A225

Timberden
Bottom

Shoreham

Meenfield
Wood

Start

Station

Dunstall
Woods

DARENT VALLEY

he unassuming River Darent squeezes through the North Downs to flow into the Thames at Dartford Marshes. This part of the valley is only a short distance from south-east London, and yet

Footbridge over River Darent.

it feels incredibly rural, which is no doubt why it has been such a popular spot with artists over the centuries.

Begin at Shoreham Station, possibly visiting the Countryside Centre located on the premises, and walk down the lane past the church into the village. At the bridge turn right into Darenth Way (the river and its valley are sometimes spelt with an additional 'h'), and pass Water House, one-time home of the 19th century landscape artist Samuel Palmer. Among regular visitors was his friend and teacher William Blake. On the hillside opposite is a huge cross carved into the chalk to commemorate those who fell in the First World War.

This tranquil, riverside route is part of the Darent Valley Path, which now switches banks via a footbridge by some attractive cottages. Go past the end of a small lane, and around and then through fields of crops to finally reach a raised path above a large hop garden (*not* called a hop field, by the way). In the summer the bines (the climbing stem) grow up strings suspended from a wire frame, and in late August the bines are stripped and the hops dried in oast kilns

INFORMATION

Distance: 11 km (6.5 miles).

Start and finish: Shoreham Station.

Terrain: Some fairly rough and steep surfaces; strong footwear advisable. Some of the walk follows waymarks for the Darent Valley Path (a boxed 'D'); and also some for the Lullingstone Country Park circular walk.

Public transport: Shoreham Station (trains from Victoria).

Refreshments: In Shoreham at the Countryside Centre and numerous pubs; and Lullingstone Park Visitor Centre.

Opening hours: Shoreham Countryside Centre, summer weekends only; Lullingstone Park Visitor Centre, daily, 1000-1700; Lullingstone Castle, weekends and bank holidays, Apr-Oct, 1400-1800; Roman Villa, daily, Apr-Oct 1000-1800, Oct-Mar 1000-1600 (admission charge); Shoreham Aircraft Museum, every Sunday, May-Sept, 1000-1700 (admission charge).

Further information: Darent Valley Path leaflet from Lullingstone Park Visitor Centre, Kingfisher Bridge, Castle Road, nr Eynsford, Kent DA4 0JF, tel 01322 865995.

Hop garden, Darent Valley.

before being sent to the brewers. Originally drying took place in the distinctive, white-coned oast houses, once so typical of rural Kent, but today nearly all these buildings have been converted into private dwellings.

Beyond the farm house join a road for 500 m, crossing carefully by Kingfisher Bridge for the entrance to Lullingstone Park Visitor Centre. This splendid site, run by Sevenoaks District Council, houses a cafe, toilets, shop and gallery, plus many educational and hands-on exhibits popular with children.

Behind the centre, continue along the cool, shaded bank of the river in the company of dragonflies and wagtails. Beyond the end of a lake is the huge brick gatehouse of Lullingstone Castle (a handsome period mansion), with a flint Norman church before it, then a lane takes you on to a Roman villa. Probably built in the first century AD, imagine the villa as a spacious country house for a wealthy Roman family, with baths, heating, and even its own Christian chapel (the only one found in a private Roman villa in Britain). Allow a minimum of half an hour for the taped tour of the covered, well-preserved remains, which include colourful mosaic tiled flooring.

Take the stepped path uphill through trees next to the villa, signposted 'Lullingstone Park circular walk'. Soon, across open fields, there are panoramic views of Eynsford and its handsome railway viaduct. Nearing the brow of the hill, follow the main path left, across a wide field. The solitary tree on your right is known as Percyvall's Sycamore, planted in 1871 to mark the birth of a local man. Go past the golf course (beware balls aiming at the green) and via a thicket and a field.

Follow red waymarks into woodland before you, then across a clearing into more, where there are three massive, gnarled oak trees. Lullingstone Park is famous for its old oaks, some having been planted when a medieval deer park was established here 700 years ago. Finally emerge and turn right, between fairways, up towards the clubhouse. Again, watch out for wayward golf balls.

Turn left at the circular walk signpost, through more trees and across another fairway. After a climb, turn right at a junction of paths, and over a high ladder stile, supposedly the highest in Kent; there's an accompanying gate for the less agile. Go across a field, left into a lane and right along a drive (public footpath). Beyond the cottages a field edge path leads to a slightly tricky double stile overlooking the beautiful Timberden Bottom, a narrow and unspoilt valley tucked away in the hills.

Follow the path down the slope and left into Cockerhurst Road, then at its end turn right, up the narrow road for Halstead (ignore the Shoreham turning). At Darenth Hulme House, turn off left for the bridleway - not the sunken path - that curves out along the top of steeply sloping fields with fabulous views over Shoreham, and towards Otford and Sevenoaks.

Fields near Shoreham.

When you are virtually level with Shoreham church, cross a stile and descend into the village. Emerging on the main street you pass the tiny Shoreham Aircraft Museum, which has relics from the Battle of Britain that was fought in these skies over 50 years ago. Turn right and then left into Church Street, which will take you back to the station.

Shoreham is full of elegant old buildings, as well as plenty of pubs. On Church Street look out for the Samuel Palmer School of Fine Art, and nearing the river the King's Arms. This fine old pub is reputed to have the only surviving ostler box left in the country. An ostler was a person employed by inns to look after customers' horses, and he waited in a little hut or box at the front of the building. The one at the King's Arms has in it a waxwork figure, the Jolly Ostler, sitting patiently with a clay pipe waiting for business.

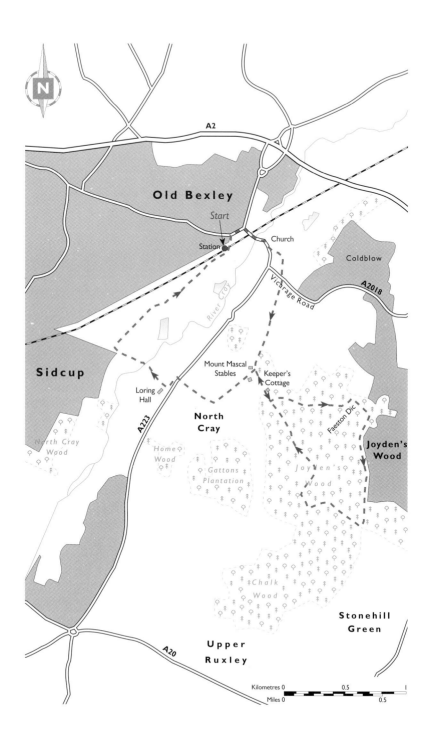

JOYDEN'S WOOD

South-east London still has some wonderful pockets of woodland, like Petts Wood and Oxleas Wood, but one of the most extensive is Joyden's Wood near Old Bexley. Continuously forested since the 16th century, the Woodland Trust purchased it from the Forestry Commission in 1987 and are gradually thinning out the conifers and non-native trees such as sycamore. Over time this will allow the indigenous types such as oak and hazel to grow more vigorously, as well as encouraging wild flowers which will in turn attract more insects and birds.

Joyden's Wood is one of over 800 that the Woodland Trust has purchased since it was founded in 1972, and in the last ten years alone it has planted over a million trees. To find out how you can help them preserve our diminishing broadleaved woodland, contact the address in the information section on page vi.

Walk along Old Bexley High Street as far as the Parish Church of St Mary. Dating originally from Norman times this handsome, shingled building with a distinctive octagonal spire also has a well-preserved lych gate, a roofed gateway to the churchyard under which coffin-bearers would wait for the clergyman to arrive before proceeding any further. Turn left into Manor Road, then right along an alleyway (indicated 'footpath'), and where it emerges with a graveyard on the left, take the short path opposite that connects with Vicarage Road.

Here you will see signs for the Cray Riverway, a short, waymarked trail that follows the River Cray from Foots Cray near Sidcup to the Thames at Erith. Cross the busy road carefully and by College Cottage enter a long, tree-lined drive that eventually leads to Mount Mascal Stables. At the far side veer left, with the forested hillside above, and at Keeper's Cottage go left again through gates into the wood.

INFORMATION

Distance: 9 km (5.5 miles).

Start and finish: Bexley Station.

Terrain: Undulating and sometimes rough woodland tracks. Strong footwear advisable. Look out for Dartford Borough Council's circular walk waymarks in the wood, and Cray Riverway signs at the beginning and end of the walk.

Public transport: Bexley Station (trains from Charing Cross); buses 132, 229, 269, 726; 492, B15 (Mon-Sat).

Refreshments: Old Bexley town centre.

Further information: Cray Riverway leaflet from Planning Dept, London Borough of Bexley, Wyncham House, 207 Longlands Road, Sidcup, Kent DA15 7JH, tel 0181 303 7777.

Sunken lane in Joyden's Wood.

After 50 m turn left off the main track for a sunken path which winds its way through the shade to the top of the hill. Go half-left at a three-way junction of tracks, and keep to this main route as it wanders through the trees. At one point it bends sharply right, and although mostly hidden this is in fact the end of a small surviving part of Faeston Dic (or dyke), a 1.8 km linear earthwork first recorded in a Saxon boundary survey of AD814 but believed to date back much further, possibly to the Battle of Crayford in AD457 when Saxon invasions followed the departure of the Romans.

Eventually you come to a junction where a signposted path goes straight on to Ferndell Avenue. Instead turn right, and follow this long, undulating track, which finally widens as a forest drive comes in from the left. This swings right and you arrive at an open, grassy picnic spot.

In addition to selective felling, the Woodland Trust is also widening some of the rides to encourage ground flora and insects; and trying to stop the spread of rhododendron, which was originally planted by the Mount Mascal Estate (they owned the woods last century) as ground cover for game birds. One inhabitant of Joyden's Wood that is native and present in great numbers is the wood ant. These large brown

A popular path.

insects can be seen marching purposefully about the forest floor, gathering material for their huge nests of twigs and pine needles. Observe them from a distance, since they sting and spray formic acid when provoked!

Turn left off the main track (behind the low ridge bordering the picnic site) and follow the path around a small, open patch that was flattened by the hurricane in 1987. Rowan, cherry and chestnut have all been planted here since then. Go back up through dense conifers and turn left onto the main forest drive once more. Follow it all the way downhill and back to Mount Mascal riding stables, but here turn sharp left and follow signs for the Cray Riverway up across a field. At the kissing gate on the brow, keep to the field edge on your right and descend to North Cray Road.

Since there is a central island for pedestrians, this busy road can be crossed here; but if a safe gap in the traffic does not materialise then take the Cray Riverway's sensible lead and turn right, along the pavement, to cross at the roundabout further on. Off the old, abandoned

St Mary's, Old Bexley, with lych gate.

road on the far side is Loring Hall, where the one-time foreign secretary Lord Castlereagh lived between 1811 and 1822.

By its side is Water Lane, which you should turn down, and at the end of this cross the River Cray by a footbridge (sign-posted Cray Riverway to Hall Place via Old Bexley). A fenced path now skirts a water pumping station; emerging between houses, turn right to join a waymarked path over farmland and then waste ground that leads to Bexley Cricket Club; after this an adjoining alleyway under the railway delivers you back to the High Street.

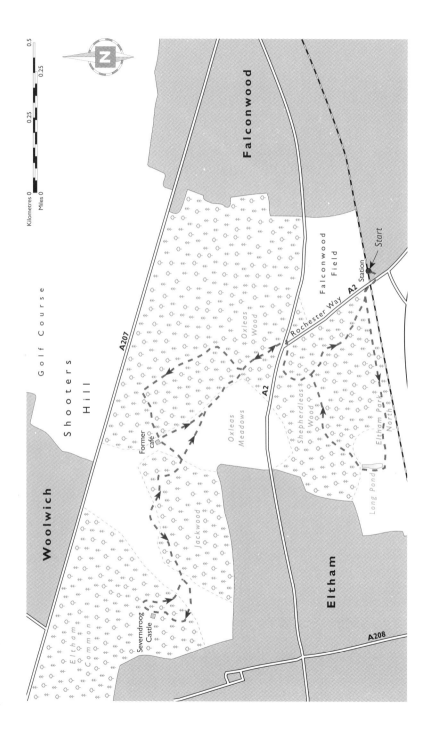

OXLEAS WOOD

Over the last 15 years there have been several well-publicised battles to halt new road-building projects, with too many (notably Twyford Down and Newbury) succumbing to the relentless drive of today's car culture. However, when plans for the new East London River Crossing emerged in the early 1990s, environmentalists and local people alike were horrified to learn that the new road was to pass through the edge of the 8,000-year-old Oxleas Wood.

It took a concerted campaign to save the 130 ha wood near Eltham, and to preserve another precious piece of green London from the jaws of the bulldozer. Go and see for yourself why so many people felt so passionately about a small wood, and try to figure out why anyone would want to lay tarmac through a Local Nature Reserve and a designated Site of Special Scientific Interest.

Turn right outside Falconwood Station and cross Rochester Way for a footpath into the woods of Eltham Park North, some of which is known as Shepherdleas Wood. For most of this walk you will be following various parts of the Green Chain Walk (GCW), a London Walking Forum-approved series of walking routes that stretch for 63 km between Thamesmead and Crystal Palace and provide a useful pedestrian link between nearly 300 open spaces in south-east London.

Take the wide track parallel with the railway; after 500 m it leaves the trees (and the din of the A2) and

INFORMATION

Distance: 5.5 km (3.5 miles) or shorter route 4 km (2.5 miles).

Start and finish: Falconwood Station.

Terrain: Easy woodland tracks. No special footwear necessary. Most of the walk follows waymarks for the Green Chain Walk ('GCW'). Accessible for pushchairs/wheelchairs.

Public transport: Falconwood Station (trains from Charing Cross); or bus B16. (Or from Shooters Hill on far side of Eltham Common buses 89, 122, 161, 178.)

Refreshments: None on route, but seasonal cafe above Oxleas Meadows may reopen.

Further information: Green Chain Walk (4 free booklets), from Dept of Planning, London Borough of Greenwich, John Humphries House, Stockwell Close, London SE10 9JN, tel 0181 854 8888.

Pointing the way.

reveals views towards the City and the high clay ridge of Forest Hill and Crystal Palace, topped by the two transmitter masts that are such a distinctive landmark for everyone 'south of the river'. Follow GCW waymarks past Long Pond and back into the woods. After 400 m turn left at a junction of tracks (indicated 'Oxleas Wood'). Soon this path emerges at a traffic light junction, where you should cross carefully, and enter Oxleas Wood opposite.

Oxleas Wood.

Follow the main track sharply right at a junction of paths, with views of an open meadow off to the left; as you go deeper into what is some of London's longest-established woodland there are plenty of smaller paths and opportunities to explore. Look out for oak, alder and birch, plus more unusual types like the lofty wild cherry and the wild service tree. Flowers include wood sage and yellow pimpernel; and among the shrubs are butcher's broom, a firm evergreen that was once sliced and used to clean butcher's chopping boards (hence its name), and the white summer flowers and translucent red berries of guelder rose.

Nuthatch, spotted flycatcher, chiffchaff and wood warbler can all be seen; but more remarkable is that Oxleas Wood supports over 100 species of butterfly and moth, almost 200 species of beetle, and 70 species of spider. Make sure to bring your wildlife identification books! After 200 m turn left at another GCW signpost (towards the Thames Barrier, not Thamesmead) and this rising path emerges by rhododendrons near the top of an open hill overlooking Oxleas Meadows, with fine views towards Sidcup and Chislehurst.

Those on the shorter walk should wait here; otherwise leave the hilltop for the path signposted 'Woolwich Common', and follow plentiful GCW posts right, up through Jackwood, then at the top left, via formal gardens and lawns, for a path back through the undergrowth at the far end. Further on there is a choice of paths, the upper one avoiding some steep steps through a terraced garden.

Both emerge at Severndroog Castle, an 18th century folly built to celebrate Sir William James' victory over Arabian pirates off the coast of Malabar in 1755. Although presently closed, the oddly-shaped but rather handsome tower was a lookout post during the last war, and indeed the views from the gardens just below should not be missed.

Severndroog Castle.

Bordering this whole area to the north is Shooters Hill, and the Romans' famous Watling Street, a route that once filled London-bound travellers from Kent with dread. The woods through which you have been walking were filled with gangs of ruffians and robbers laying in wait for passing stagecoaches. Passengers had to carry pistols, and it was not unusual to see a highwayman swinging from one of the many gibbets lining the steep road.

From the tower you can continue across Eltham Common to Shooters Hill for bus connections; or return along one of the alternative paths via Jackwood to Oxleas Meadows, but instead of climbing back up the hill, head straight across the middle of the wide grassy area, making for the small brick shelter on the far side. Here you will be met by the shorter route, coming down from the hilltop.

Follow the surfaced track behind the shelter into the woods and at a junction of tracks take the ahead/right fork rather than the two paths leftwards, and so rejoin your original outward route. Recross the main road by the lights and re-enter the trees, and then at the GCW signpost deep in Shepherdleas Wood go straight over, and this will return you to Falconwood.

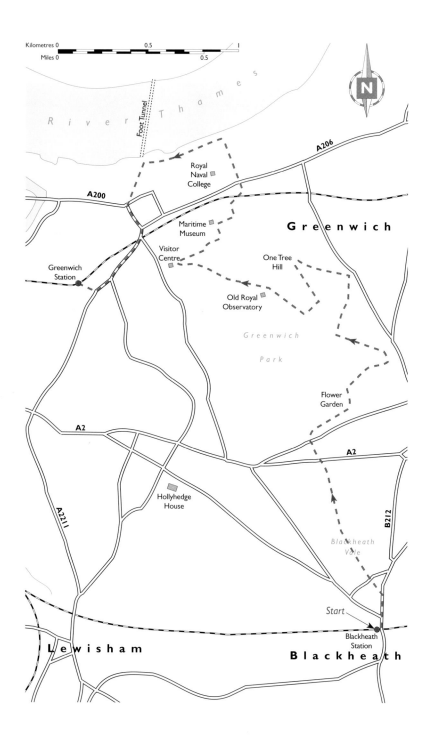

Kilometres 0   0.5   1
Miles 0   0.5

N

River Thames

Foot Tunnel

A206

A200

Royal Naval College

Maritime Museum

G r e e n w i c h

Visitor Centre

Greenwich Station

One Tree Hill

Old Royal Observatory

Greenwich Park

Flower Garden

A2

A2

A211

Hollyhedge House

B212

Blackheath Vale

Start

L e w i s h a m

Blackheath Station

B l a c k h e a t h

BLACKHEATH AND GREENWICH

G reenwich offers such a wealth of visitor attractions that this comparatively short walk through some of the oldest enclosed Royal parkland will likely prove a day-long outing. Also, since parking is often tricky at both start and finish, let the train take the strain or the bus take the fuss.

Turn left out of Blackheath Station and fork right into Montpelier Vale, then continue via the handsome All Saints parish church to the heath. Today it is no more than a vast, open grassy space criss-crossed by roads and home to kite-fliers, joggers and occasional funfairs. But once it was a wild, dangerous place for unaccompanied travellers on the Dover to London road. It was also from here in 1381 that Wat Tyler led 10,000 protesters from Kent into London as the Peasants' Revolt against the new poll tax reached its climax; and in 1415 crowds massed on the heath to welcome the victorious Henry V back from Agincourt.

Aim for the tree-topped wall of Greenwich Park ahead, with the pointed cap of Canary Wharf blinking away beyond like a giant space rocket waiting to take off (low cloud permitting). Cross Shooters Hill Road by the lights, then once through Blackheath Gate, turn right into the Flower Garden. There are over 30 colourful beds, plus a landscaped lake and, through the trees to the right, a deer enclosure with viewpoints. (Those with dogs will have to walk around the outside of the Flower Garden.)

INFORMATION

Distance: 5.5 km (3.5 miles).

Start: Blackheath Station.

Finish: Greenwich Station.

Terrain: Easy, mostly surfaced paths. No special footwear necessary. Accessible for pushchairs/ wheelchairs.

Public transport: Both stations are on the Charing Cross/London Bridge line. To Blackheath, buses 54, 89, 108, 202, 306; from Greenwich, buses 177, 180, 188, 199, 286, 386, and riverboats to/from Westminster Pier.

Refreshments: numerous pubs and cafes in Blackheath and Greenwich, plus tearooms in Greenwich Park near Royal Observatory and at the Visitor Centre by St Mary's Gate.

Opening times: Greenwich Park, daily, dawn to dusk; Royal Observatory and Planetarium, National Maritime Museum (grounds free), Queen's House, Cutty Sark, all daily, 1000-1700 (admission charges); Greenwich Park Visitor Centre, daily 1000-1700.

Flower beds, Greenwich Park.

With the lake on your left turn right, to Vanbrugh Park Gate, then return either along the edge of the garden or the walkway outside it. From the latter you can begin to appreciate the original park layout. Geometric avenues of oak, elm, lime and sweet chestnut were planted as long ago as the mid 17th century; and among the 3,000 trees in the park is the world's oldest, the Gingko (fossilised remains date it from the Jurassic era, 150 million years ago). A specimen can be found by the visitor centre, further on.

At the junction of tracks towards the centre of the park turn right, past the fenced-off site of a Roman villa, and at Maze Hill Gate take the second left to One Tree Hill, with views of the Thames and Docklands. Now follow the path downhill by the railings and at the bottom cross Lovers Walk for the path up behind the old drinking fountain, passing an ancient fallen tree known as Queen Elizabeth's Oak. Elizabeth I supposedly played inside the 2m-wide trunk; and later the hollow tree was used to imprison offenders who had fallen foul of park rules!

At the top of the hill turn left for the cafe; or ahead for the huge statue of General Wolfe. His view is superlative: below, the park stretches down to the stately buildings of the Maritime Museum and Royal Naval College, and beyond the looping Thames are

A view of Docklands.

the dynamic shapes of the new offices and flats of Dockland, with Canary Wharf centre-stage. Next to you on the hilltop is the elegant Royal Observatory, designed by Wren in 1675. A brass strip across the courtyard is where the Meridian line divides eastern and western hemispheres (zero longitude) - the classic pose for the camera is to stand with a foot in each.

Walk down the steep track from the Observatory to the Park visitor centre and tearoom by St Mary's Gate. Then, staying in the park, walk past the statue of King William IV and into the grounds of the National Maritime Museum. Go along the grand colonnade to the Queen's House, designed by Inigo Jones for James I, and eventually make for the gate in the far corner by the display of giant old anchors, including one from the Royal Navy's last conventional aircraft carrier *Ark Royal*.

Cross Romney Road and walk down Park Row to the river. By the appropriately-named Trafalgar Tavern, turn left on to the Thames Path and follow the narrow riverside walkway beside the railings of the Royal Naval College. Greenwich Palace once stood near here, birthplace of Henry VIII, Mary I and Elizabeth I, but it was demolished by the Stuarts. The stately buildings you see today were begun around 1700 as a hospital for injured seamen, but in 1873 the Royal Naval College moved here from Portsmouth; and shortly the University of Greenwich is to take over the site.

The waterfront at Greenwich is dominated by the *Cutty Sark*, that most handsome of sailing ships. The only survivor of the famous clippers, she regularly raced across the seas with tea from the East and later wool from Australia, and could cover over 560 km (350 miles) on a good day. Tiny by comparison but also in dry dock near the pier, *Gypsy Moth IV* is the yacht in which Sir Francis Chichester became the first man to sail around the world single-handed, in 1966/67. He was knighted by the Queen here at Greenwich.

Royal Naval College.

If you want to continue beyond Greenwich, consider the foot tunnel to Island Gardens, the Thames Path either upstream to Deptford and Rotherhithe or downstream to the Thames Barrier; and there is always the option of a boat trip to end the day. Otherwise walk up Church Street and along the High Road to the railway station.

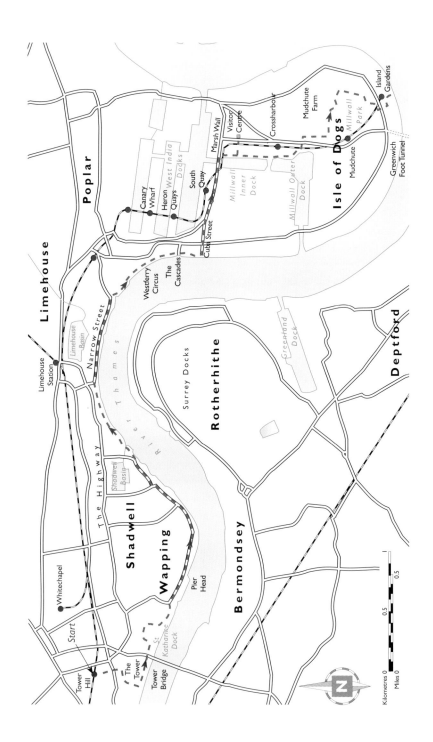

DOCKLANDS

This journey into the heart of modern London begins at one of the oldest sites of all. Outside Tower Hill station is a huge sundial with a chronological history of the capital carved around its base, and below is the subway to the Tower of London. Since William the Conqueror built the original Tower after defeating Harold more than 900 years ago, this royal fortress/prison has held a central place in English history - not least because legend says that if the resident ravens leave, the kingdom will fall!

Turn right and walk around the moat to the main entrance and waterfront, opposite HMS *Belfast*, and past Traitor's Gate for a short tunnel underneath the approach to the mighty Tower Bridge. Return to the river by a striking statue of a girl with a dolphin; then go across the entrance of St Katharine Dock before turning left for a closer look at the Thames sailing barges and yachts tied up in the renovated basin.

Facing you is Dickens Inn, a modern structure that does actually contain some original 18th century timbers, named after the writer who described life in the docks of the East End in such vivid detail. At your feet, now preserved on the quay, is Telford's original footbridge which once spanned the dock entrance. Turn right and walk down to and then along St Katharine's Way between the former warehouses. A Thames Path sign directs you to a new river terrace, with views of Butler's Wharf opposite, then back to Wapping High Street.

Continue for some way, past the attractive Georgian houses of Wapping Pierhead, built for London Dock Company officials between 1811-13, and on to the Town of Ramsgate. A small, dark but highly inviting pub, typical of old Wapping, this was where the notorious Judge Jeffreys was caught preparing to escape after the Glorious Revolution of 1688; and later it was renamed in honour of the thirsty Kent fishermen who landed their catch nearby. It may be hard to believe

INFORMATION

Distance: 10.5 km (6.5 miles).

Start: Tower Hill tube station.

Finish: Island Gardens.

Terrain: Mostly easy, surfaced paths. Accessible for wheelchairs/pushchairs (but some steps). Follow Thames Path waymarks.

Public transport: Tower Hill tube station (Circle and District lines, Docklands Light Railway), buses 15, 25 (weekends), 100, D1 (Mon-Fri); Island Gardens station (Docklands Light Railway), buses D7, D8 (Mon-Sat), P14, and riverboats from Greenwich to Westminster.

Refreshments: Numerous pubs and cafes; see *The Special Charm of Waterside Pubs in London Docklands*, available from Docklands Visitor Centre.

Opening hours: Tower of London, daily, 0930-1700 (admission charge); Docklands Visitor Centre, 3 Limeharbour, Isle of Dogs, London E14 9TQ, tel 0171 512 1111, daily, 0830-1800 (Mon-Fri), 0930-1700 (weekends).

today, but at one time Wapping High Street boasted 36 pubs! A little further on is another, the Captain Kidd, whose courtyard sports its very own hangman's noose and a bar known as The Gallows (ex-naval officer turned pirate Kidd was executed near here in 1701).

Continue down the High Street, past the tube station, and after another brief burst of new riverside turn right, along Wapping Wall. Turn right again, after the Prospect of Whitby, built around 1520 and claiming to be London's oldest riverside inn; then cross the

London's oldest riverside inn.

entrance to Shadwell Basin by the lift bridge and walk back out to the riverside via a small park.

Eventually go through a courtyard and turn right on to The Highway, a noisy road full of traffic disappearing into the Limehouse Link Tunnel. Mercifully you also depart very soon, down Narrow Street, leading to

Limehouse Basin. Here the Regent's Canal meets the Thames after its journey through north London, and the Limehouse Cut connects with the southern end of the Lea Valley Walk at Bow. Further on a new park has been laid out at Ropemakers' Field, a name that reflects the area's former activities.

Indeed, 'Limehouse' itself comes from the one-time abundance of limekilns, where Kentish chalk was burnt for use in the building trade. Next to the park is a pub called The House They Left Behind (you'll see why). Opposite this, follow Thames Path signs

Thames Path, Limehouse.

through Duke Shore Wharf for a new waterside path, with fresh views downstream as the river loops around the Isle of Dogs.

All around you new developments continue to spring up, as the great urban renewal programme initiated in the early 1980s rolls on. As elsewhere, the former wharves and warehouses of the Limehouse waterfront have been replaced or converted into stylish flats and apartments. The old docks have been totally transformed: Surrey Docks, across the river, now includes a small nature reserve and farm, and an artificial, 20 m-high hill; while ahead of you the former West India Docks, built between 1800-06 and a bustling commercial centre for over 150 years, is now the site of Heron Quays and Canary Wharf, the centrepiece of today's new Docklands.

For a closer look, turn left at Canary Wharf Pier and go up the steps to Westferry Circus and along West India Avenue to Canada Square and Canary Wharf. Designed by Cesar Pelli (who was also responsible for the World Trade Center in New York), Britain's tallest building is 240 m high, has 50 floors, and is a truly awesome construction - already an instantly recognisable landmark for London.

The Cascades, Docklands.

Back on the riverside, continue past the Cascades residential development and turn left into Cuba Street. At the junction with Westferry Road the Thames Path heads right, but you should cross over and continue until Cuba Street bends right. Go up the steps in front of you and turn right on to Marsh Wall, with fantastic views of Canary Wharf and the trains of the elevated Docklands Light Railway shuttling in and out of its base.

Go past South Quay Station and under the railway, then turn right

on the far side of Millwall Inner Dock to reach
Harbour Exchange Square and two preserved 'Sputnik'
cranes, so-called because of their resemblance to the
rockets that launched the Russian satellite in the
1950s. Here turn left and cross Limeharbour for a short
detour to the Docklands Visitor Centre, where you
can learn what the working docks were really like; and
about the incredible variety of goods imported - from
tobacco to sugar, scents and perfumes to wool (as late
as the early 1960s nearly a million bales a year still
came through London's docks from Australia and New
Zealand).

Resume your dockside walk, past Glengall Bridge, and
at some wide waterside steps turn left on a path
signposted 'East Ferry Road'. Go under the railway,
across the road, and up steps to reach the top of a
grassy embankment, which soon bears left. (If the steps
or gradient are a problem, continue down East Ferry
Road to Island Gardens.) Rope-laying machines
running on rails once used this seemingly odd,
elevated location, and today it provides an excellent
vantage point - Canary Wharf and central Docklands
one way and Greenwich the other.

Below are allotments and Mudchute City Farm, the
largest urban farm in Europe. The name Mudchute, by
the way, comes from the huge amount of dredged mud
deposited here during the building of Millwall Docks.
Above the riding school, go down steps to turn left on
to a second embankment; then descend to a green
metal swing gate and take the track behind the One
o'clock Club around the outer edge of Millwall Park.

Leave the park at the far end, near the viaduct, and
cross the road to Island Gardens station. Go down
Ferry Street, left into Saunders Ness Road, and on
your right are the lawns and plane trees of Island
Gardens itself, with superb views across to Wren's
handsome Greenwich waterfront (see Walk 11). If you
don't wish to return on the Docklands Light Railway,
then take the foot tunnel for a free and unique
subterranean river crossing to Greenwich.

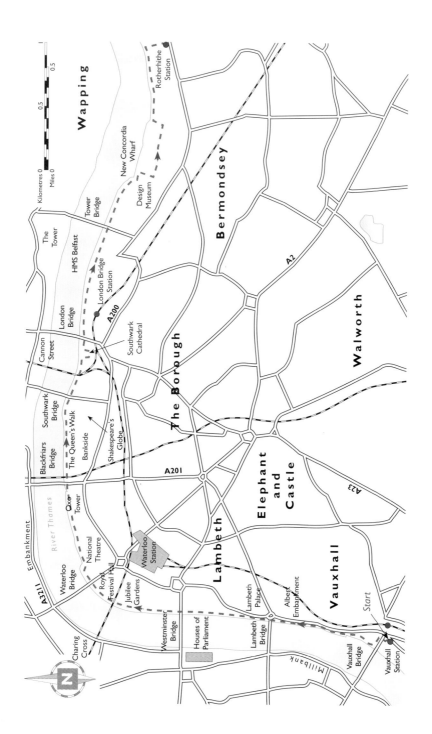

Wapping

New Concordia Wharf

Tower Bridge

Design Museum

Rotherhithe Station

Bermondsey

A2

The Tower

London Bridge

HMS Belfast

London Bridge Station

A200

Southwark Cathedral

Cannon Street

The Borough

Walworth

Southwark Bridge

Blackfriars Bridge

The Queen's Walk

Bankside

Shakespeare's Globe

A201

Oxo Tower

Elephant and Castle

A23

Embankment

River Thames

National Theatre

Waterloo Bridge

Royal Festival Hall

Waterloo Station

Jubilee Gardens

Lambeth

Lambeth Palace

Albert Embankment

Vauxhall

Start

A3211

Charing Cross

Westminster Bridge

Houses of Parliament

Lambeth Bridge

Vauxhall Bridge

Vauxhall Station

Millbank

Kilometres 0   0.5
Miles 0   0.5

N

SOUTH BANK

This stroll along the Thames in central London offers endless attractions: the South Bank Centre, Shakespeare's Globe, Southwark Cathedral, Tower Bridge, the Design Museum, and much more. There are excellent public transport connections all the way along; waymarks for the new Thames Path National Trail are in good supply; and you may be surprised that a recreational walk in a city centre doesn't have to involve endless pavement walking amid noise and car fumes.

Leave Vauxhall tube station/subway by Exit 6 ('Albert Embankment (riverside)') and take the footbridge over the ceaseless traffic and up to Vauxhall Bridge. The mammoth, yellow and green building that dominates everything was designed by Terry Farrell and is the new HQ for MI6 - hardly inconspicuous! Opposite, Eurostar trains rumble past on their way into Waterloo from Paris and Brussels. There are steps down from Vauxhall Bridge to the smart riverside terrace, which leads to the Albert Embankment.

Go beneath Lambeth Bridge, and to your right is Lambeth Palace, London home of the Archbishop of Canterbury, and next door the former Church of St Mary, now a museum of garden history. Turning your attention the other way, the Houses of Parliament rise impressively on the far bank, the classic view that forms the backdrop to so many TV news reports. But the Gothic spires designed by Barry and Pugin date only from the 1830s, after the original was largely destroyed by fire.

Ahead, the tree-lined embankment loses the traffic behind St Thomas's Hospital, which moved here in 1871 after 800 years on its original site near London Bridge; and which today includes the Florence Nightingale Museum. Take the subway under Westminster Bridge Road and past the former County Hall to reach Jubilee Gardens and the South Bank complex. Hungerford Bridge stretches starkly out

INFORMATION

Distance: 8 km (5 miles).

Start: Vauxhall Station.

Finish: Rotherhithe Station.

Terrain: Easy, surfaced paths all the way. Follow waymarks for the Thames Path. Accessible for pushchairs/wheelchairs after South Bank (steps at Vauxhall and Westminster).

Public transport: Vauxhall tube station (Victoria line) or railway station (trains from Waterloo); buses 2, 36, 44, 77, 77A, 88, 185, 344; Rotherhithe tube station (East London line); buses P11, P14, and 47, 188 from Jamaica Road.

Refreshments: Countless!

Opening hours: Museum of Garden History, Mar-Dec, Mon-Fri 1030-1600, Sun 1030-1700; Shakespeare's Globe, exhibition/daily tours, 1000-1700 (admission charge); Clink Prison Museum, daily, 1000-1600 (admission charge); HMS *Belfast,* daily, 1000-1700 (admission charge); Tower Bridge, daily, 1000-1830 Apr-Oct, 1000-1600 Nov-Mar (admission charge); Design Museum, Mon-Fri 1130-1800, Sat/Sun 1200-1800 (admission charge).

across the rather murky river to the modernistic shape of Charing Cross Station.

As you proceed along Queen's Walk you may notice engraved aluminium discs appearing at intervals between the paving stones. These mark the route of

View from Queen's Walk to the City.

the Silver Jubilee Walkway, a 20 km circular route around central London starting at Lambeth Bridge which was created to celebrate the Queen's Silver Jubilee in 1977. Above you, the uncompromising concrete and glass edifice of the Royal Festival Hall is the focus for the largest arts complex in Europe, which also includes the Hayward Gallery and the Museum of the Moving Image, plus the National Theatre and National Film Theatre - which you pass next. From the skateboarders and second-hand booksellers underneath Waterloo Bridge, continue along the riverside to Gabriel's Wharf, a small and unexpected area of cafes and colourful craft shops which is well worth pausing over.

Carrying on along the riverfront, there are absorbing views across to the City, plus all the activity on the river itself: barges, sightseeing boats, the riverbus, and so on. You pass beneath the colourful crest of the London, Chatham and Dover Railway, which steamed into Blackfriars Station for the first time in 1863; once under the bridge, the symmetrical if stark shapes of Bankside power station hit you. Designed by Sir Giles Gilbert Scott (also behind the Battersea model - see Walk 14) the vast brick walls and rigid angles, culminating in the colossal main chimney, provide a fascinating

River walk, South Bank (towards St Paul's).

juxtaposition to the graceful dome and fine detail of Wren's St Paul's Cathedral that you can see on the opposite bank. The redundant power station will soon hold the Tate Gallery's collection of modern art.

Now you must turn the clock back even further for one of the walk's highlights - Shakespeare's Globe Theatre. In Elizabethan London, if you wanted bawdy entertainment you went to Southwark: taverns and brothels, bear-baiting and cock-fighting, plus four playhouses where the latest works by Shakespeare and others were rowdily received. In 1613 the Globe burnt down after a spark from a cannon that was being used in a performance of *Henry VIII* set the thatch roof alight; but now recreated in almost exact detail - the plaster walls are made from sand, goat's hair and lime - the Globe offers tours as well as regular performances that give you a chance to sample Shakespearean drama in its original format.

The Thames Path continues under Southwark Bridge, where murals describe the Frost Fairs once held on the frozen river; then, beyond the 18th century Anchor Inn, go under the railway to reach the site of the former Clink Prison. Today an exhibition tells the story of the original 'clink': 'For almost 300 years The Clink held martyrs, debtors, whores, thieves and even actors. Now it's your turn...' The prison was established by the Bishops of Winchester, who controlled 'the Liberty of the Clink', and further along Clink Street you pass the excavated remains of their palace.

Beyond the docked schooner, *Kathleen & May*, Southwark Cathedral suddenly appears through a gap in the crowded buildings. This has been a site of worship for over 1,000 years. Chaucer's pilgrims assembled in Southwark; and William Shakespeare, who was a regular visitor, is commemorated inside (his youngest brother, Edmund, is buried here). Today the cathedral remains an oasis of calm amid the hurly-burly of SE1.

Go to the left of the cathedral, past the chapter house, and under London Bridge along Tooley Street. Within 100 m a fingerpost points you back to the riverfront, and along to Hay's Galleria. This former wharf is now covered and converted to hold cafes, shops and a wonderful nautical sculpture by David Kemp called *The Navigators*, which every now and then starts moving and spouts water.

Ahead are three famous landmarks associated with the Thames in London. In the foreground is HMS *Belfast*, veteran cruiser of the Second World War; then further on is Tower Bridge, with the Tower of London on the

River walk, towards HMS *Belfast*.

far bank. If you want to visit the latter, or simply shorten the walk, cross here and finish at Tower Hill tube station. The well-known bridge, opened in 1894 and originally raised by powerful steam engines, still occasionally lifts for high-masted vessels; and an on-site exhibition has more details (entrance on Tower Bridge Road).

Go under the road and along Shad Thames, squeezing between dark, converted spice warehouses connected high above by narrow iron walkways. This is Butler's Wharf, the largest on the river when completed in 1871. Cut back through to a river terrace lined with chic cafes and restaurants. Now with Tower Bridge and the City offices mostly behind you, the widening Thames is no longer lined by cranes and wharves but stylish modern conversions. Before you is the dazzling white-walled Design Museum, with displays of 20th century consumer objects; and on the other side of Shad Thames is the Bramah Tea and Coffee Museum, located where once the tea trade flourished.

Go past the Museum and over St Saviour's footbridge to New Concordia Wharf, then through a narrow opening to turn right, then shortly left, into Jacob Street. (If in any doubt follow the Thames Path signs, since considerable building work is taking place along this Bermondsey stretch and it is likely that the route may change.) At the end go ahead into Chambers Street, then left into Loftie Street and across Fountain Green Square to regain the river. Partly riverside and well-signposted pavement, the final stage into Rotherhithe is easy to follow, even passing the moated outline of Edward III's manor house.

Go down Rotherhithe Street to the Mayflower pub, built in the 17th century and named after the Pilgrim Fathers' famous ship which was moored near here. They left Rotherhithe in 1620 on their epic journey, and the captain, Christopher Jones, and some of the crew are buried in St Mary's Church behind you. To finish, turn right down Railway Avenue for Rotherhithe Station.

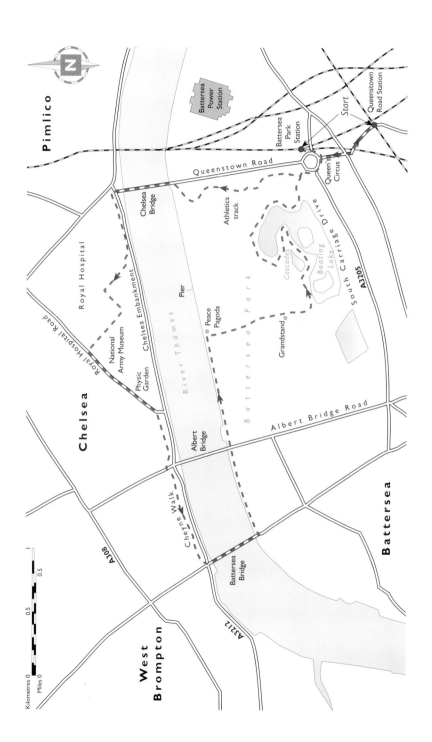

BATTERSEA PARK AND CHELSEA

Battersea Park is signposted from both stations, along Queenstown Road, and you enter it at Queen's Circus, then turn immediately right onto a footpath. This runs alongside 'The Wilderness', part of Battersea Park Local Nature Reserve, and a free Nature Trail leaflet is available from the interpretation centre at the Pump House. At the athletics track, keep to the main path around its end; beyond this, the path curves up a small hill past The Meadow, an extension of the nature reserve.

Battersea Park and the distant power station.

The rigid, distinctive shapes of Battersea power station dominate the scene, an awe-inspiring building of truly enormous proportions. Designed by Sir Giles Gilbert Scott in the early 1930s for the London Power Company, its huge chimneys were fitted with sulphur extractors to reduce pollution. It ceased operating in 1984, since when a number of plans have been put forward to convert this listed building to another use. At the time of writing all have fallen through, and the structure is starting to suffer serious neglect.

Go straight ahead and turn left out of the park, and over Chelsea Bridge. Cross the busy Chelsea Embankment via the pedestrian crossing and turn left. The memorial on the corner is to the men of the 6th Dragoon Guards (known as the Carabiniers), who fought in the South African War of 1899-1902. Almost immediately turn right into the well-tended

INFORMATION

Distance: 6.5 km (4 miles).

Start and finish: Battersea Park or Queenstown Road railway stations, or Carriage Drive South car park (enter via Queen's Circus).

Terrain: Surfaced park tracks and pavements. Accessible for pushchairs/ wheelchairs.

Public transport: Battersea Park Station (Victoria trains) and Queenstown Road (Waterloo trains); buses 44, 137, 137A, 344, and from Albert Bridge Road 49, 249 (Sun), 319, 345.

Refreshments: Lakeside cafe in Battersea Park, open daily; King's Head & Eight Bells pub, Cheyne Walk.

Opening hours: Battersea Park, daily, 0600 to dusk; National Army Museum, daily, 1000-1730 (admission charge); Physic Garden, Sun 1400-1600, Wed 1400-1700, Apr-Oct (admission charge), access via Swan Walk; Carlyle's House, March-Oct, admission charge (free to National Trust members).

Note: The Royal Hospital grounds are closed during the annual Chelsea Flower Show in May.

gardens of the Chelsea Royal Hospital. Founded by Charles II and designed by Wren, the Hospital is a home for veteran soldiers - the famous Chelsea Pensioners - with their distinctive scarlet and blue uniforms.

Some of the Hospital grounds are out of bounds to dogs; and for four days in May it is all closed to the public when the Royal Horticultural Society hold the annual Chelsea Flower Show here. If you are hindered by either, simply carry on along the Embankment to Swan Walk. Otherwise head over to the left of the handsome building, whose Chapel, Great Hall and Museum are open to visitors at certain times (enquire at the main gate).

Turn left on to Royal Hospital Road, and pass the National Army Museum, which has on display outside a large chunk of the Berlin Wall that the Royal Logistic Corps brought back from Germany in 1989. A little further on is the Physic Garden, established in 1673 and one of the oldest botanical gardens in Europe. The first cotton fields in the USA came from seeds originally grown in these gardens.

Henry Moore Statue, Battersea Park.

Cross Royal Hospital Road and enter Cheyne Walk. This smart, tree-lined street is typical of fashionable and artistic Chelsea. The terraced row of tall and handsome houses is liberally scattered with blue plaques, indicating that people of note once lived there. Pre-Raphaelites Dante Gabriel Rossetti and Algernon Charles Swinburne lived at No 16, and the Victorian novelist George Eliot died at No 4. Mrs Gaskell, Hilaire Belloc, Lloyd George and the American artist James McNeill Whistler also lived in the street at various times. Look out for the tiny Cheyne Mews, where Henry VIII's manor house once stood.

Cross over the traffic light junction opposite Albert Bridge and continue past the King's Head & Eight Bells, a pub once popular with the Victorian writer and historian Thomas Carlyle, whose nearby house at 24 Cheyne Row is now owned by the National Trust and is open to the public. A little further on is Chelsea Old Church, outside which is a statue of Sir Thomas More who once lived near here. Beyond Roper's Garden (also connected with More), cross the Embankment at the traffic lights for Battersea Bridge. Upstream is Chelsea Wharf, where the restored warehouses contrast with the new dockside flats in the distance.

Cross the river and join the riverside path on the south bank, as it makes its way downstream beneath gleaming new offices and flats. Cross Albert Bridge Road and re-enter the oasis of Battersea Park. Not that the park is surrounded by desert, of course, but when it opened in 1858 it was only the second purpose-built public park in an increasingly crowded and polluted city (the first was Victoria Park in Hackney). It has been popular with south Londoners ever since, and there are a range of attractions for just about everyone, from a children's zoo and sports pitches to formal gardens, established for the Festival of Britain in 1951.

Walk along the tree-lined riverside as far as the remarkable peace pagoda, built in 1985 by the Japanese Buddhist order Nipponzan. Turn right, into the centre of the park, and walk on past the children's zoo and the bandstand, and then take the second path on the left after the bowling green. This will take you

through the Cascades, an area of landscaped hillside full of waterfalls and shrubs (I always liken it to a giant rockery). Follow this on to the Pump House, whose art gallery and small interpretation centre is open Wed-Sun,

Peace Pagoda, Battersea Park.

and then continue around the boating lake to finish with a well-earned pot of tea or ice cream at the cafe overlooking the water.

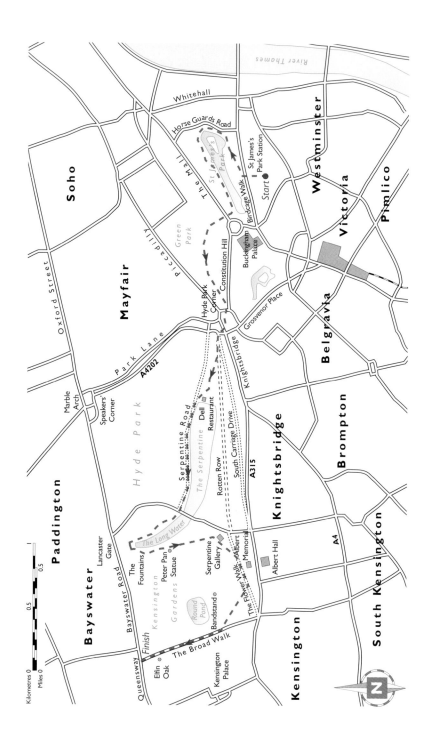

THE ROYAL PARKS

This walk takes in all four central London royal parks: St James's Park, Green Park, Hyde Park and Kensington Gardens. They began as a private hunting ground for the Tudors, but today provide a priceless area of calm and retreat amid a bustling city.

From St James's Park station cross Petty France for Queen Anne's Gate opposite, and take the narrow cut-through ahead to cross into St James's Park. Turn right, along the inner path by the flower beds that leads around the eastern end of the lake. Huddled below the imposing bulk of the Whitehall ministries across Horse Guards Road is the sandbagged entry to the Cabinet War Rooms, from where Churchill directed operations during World War II; and further

INFORMATION

Distance: 7.5 km (4.5 miles).

Start: St James's Park tube station.

Finish: Queensway tube station.

Terrain: Easy, surfaced paths. Accessible for pushchairs/ wheelchairs.

Public transport: St James's Park tube station (Circle and District lines) and buses from Victoria Street 11, 24, 211, 507 (Mon-Fri); Queensway tube station (Central line) and buses 12, 70, 94.

Refreshments: The Cake House, St James's Park; The Dell, Hyde Park; The Orangery, Kensington Gardens; plus numerous pubs/cafes in Queensway and Notting Hill Gate.

Opening hours: Parks daily, dawn to dusk; Cabinet War Rooms, daily, 1000-1800 (admission charge); Serpentine Gallery closed until end of 1997 for refurbishment; Kensington Palace State Apartments, daily, 1015-1515, May-Dec (admission charge).

Birdlife in St James's Park.

along is the wide courtyard of Horse Guards Parade, where the Queen marks her official birthday each year by Trooping the Colour.

Walk back along the far side of the lake past the Cake House cafe towards Buckingham Palace. Detour a moment to admire the magnificent views from the centre of the footbridge - of the Palace one way and what the official royal parks guide calls 'the fairytown skyline' of Whitehall the other. The lake, and Duck Island in particular, is a haven for birdlife, including black swans, ornamental ducks and even pelicans.

Much of this dates from the ornithological tendencies of Charles II, who appointed a birdkeeper and established an aviary by what is still known as Birdcage Walk. Pelicans first appeared on the lake in the late 1660s, a present to Charles II from the Russian Ambassador, and since then they have been ever-present, the latest additions being two Eastern Whites from Prague Zoo in 1995. They are fed fish every afternoon, and visitors are urged not to throw them bread and other offerings which can be dangerous to their health.

At the end of the lake, turn right and cross The Mall at the lights, with Buckingham Palace on your left. Until George IV moved here, originally the site of a house built by the Duke of Buckingham, monarchs as far back as Henry VIII had lived at St James's Palace, opposite the park (it is still the official royal court). Now go into Green Park via the arresting Canada Memorial, which records the efforts of Canadian servicemen in the two World Wars.

Follow surfaced paths into the middle of this pleasant if unspectacular leafy park and head half-left for the Green Park subway into the centre of Hyde Park Corner. You emerge near the imposing bulk of the Wellington Arch, surrounded by a constant roar from the swirling vehicles. A statue of the Iron Duke on horseback looks on in resignation, probably waiting for a gap in the traffic.

Take the Hyde Park Corner subway and, making sure to follow the arrows for Hyde Park, surface parkside of the huge junction and cross South Carriage Drive and the sandy horse ride called Rotten Row to head into Hyde Park. 'Rotten Row' is thought to come from 'Route de Roi' (the Royal Road), since this was William III's riding route from Kensington Palace to Whitehall. Oil lamps were hung in the trees along its course to deter highwaymen and robbers, supposedly the first instance of street lighting in England.

Go half-left, through the recently-restored Rose Garden, and on to the Dell Restaurant, a well-positioned cafe enjoying splendid views down the

The Serpentine, Hyde Park.

length of the Serpentine, and altogether a great place to pause for mid-walk refreshment. Proceed along the right-hand (north) bank of the Serpentine, formed in 1730 by the damming of the now-forgotten Westbourne River. Paddle-boating and duck-feeding will likely be happening one side, with roller-bladers and cyclists humming along the wide but vehicle-free roadway on the other.

Since James I allowed his subjects into Hyde Park it has been a popular spot. In fact it is the only open place in central London where the public is allowed to go horse-riding. Mass rallies and open-air concerts happen here; and away to your right at Marble Arch is Speakers' Corner, where since 1872 members of the public have stood on their soapboxes (now short stepladders) and held forth on just about anything that takes their fancy.

Stick to the waterside and go underneath the road bridge into Kensington Gardens, originally intended as the private domain of Kensington Palace but now considered part of Hyde Park. Continue to the Italianate gardens known as the Fountains at the head of the Long Water. *Lancaster Gate tube station is just across Bayswater Road.* Return along the far bank, pausing at Sir George Frampton's bronze statue of Peter Pan, its corners worn smooth by the eager hands of countless children; and a little after this take the path half-right indicated Serpentine Gallery. No Tate or National this, but a former brick tearoom that is now home to exhibitions of modern art.

From the back of the gallery head half-right on a path to the Albert Memorial, a grand and imposing monument to the Prince Consort that sits opposite another, the Albert Hall. At present the Memorial is undergoing renovation and is covered up, but a visitor centre at its foot has more details. Behind it is a sheltered passage known as the Flower Walk, with colourful flower beds and tame squirrels that will take food from your hand. Walk down this as far as the first gate (or further, if you are keen), and turn into the park in order to go half-left at a path junction and via the bandstand to turn right on to the Broad Walk.

Next to this popular promenade gulls wheel and cry above the Round Pond, and there are distant views of the West End; while on your left is Kensington Palace, developed by William III and still a royal residence. Queen Victoria, remembered by her daughter's marble statue outside, was born here; and the Sunken Gardens and Orangery (now serving afternoon teas), plus the State Apartments, are all worth visiting.

Continue along the Broad Walk to finish at Queensway (or Notting Hill Gate if you prefer). Just before you leave the park is a children's playground, and beside it is the Elfin Oak, a 600-year-old stump that was transferred from Richmond Park in 1930. Artist Ivor Innes, and latterly comedian Spike Milligan, have carved dozens of colourful creatures and figures into the gnarled old bark. How many can you spot?

St James's Park Lake.

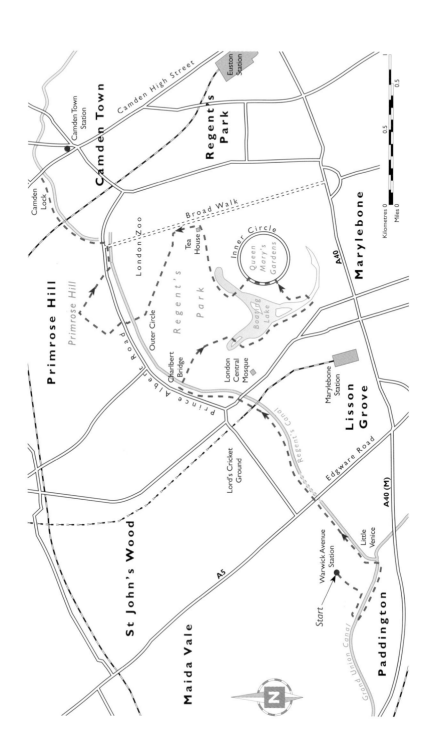

Camden Town

Euston Station

Camden Town Station

Camden High Street

Regent's Park

Camden Lock

Broad Walk

London Zoo

Tea House

Inner Circle

Queen Mary's Gardens

Marylebone

A40

Primrose Hill

Primrose Hill

Regent's Park

Outer Circle

Boating Lake

Charlbert Bridge

Prince Albert Road

London Central Mosque

Marylebone Station

Lisson Grove

Lord's Cricket Ground

Regent's Canal

Edgware Road

A40 (M)

St John's Wood

Maida Vale

A5

Little Venice

Warwick Avenue Station

Start

Grand Union Canal

Paddington

Kilometres 0   0.5
Miles 0   0.5

REGENT'S CANAL AND REGENT'S PARK

This is an easy walk full of interest: a fascinating canal that leads to a royal park, plus a zoo and hilltop views, and ending with trendy lockside markets and cafes. And all accessible by public transport.

Signs outside Warwick Avenue tube station point you up Warwick Avenue itself to the canal, but for a more interesting route go along Clifton Villas and right into Blomfield Road, crossing near the Paddington Stop (a

INFORMATION

Distance: 7.5 km (4.5 miles).

Start: Warwick Avenue tube station.

Finish: Camden Lock.

Terrain: Easy, surfaced paths. Moderately accessible for pushchairs/ wheelchairs (one easy footbridge and two flights of steps).

Public transport: Warwick Avenue (Bakerloo line) and Camden Town (Northern line); buses (start) 6, 18, 46, (finish) 24, 27, 29, 31, 134, 135, 168, 214, 253, 274, C2.

Refreshments: Numerous, but note especially the Waterside Cafe at Little Venice, Cafe Laville above Maida Hill tunnel, the Rose Garden Buffet in Regent's Park, and the market cafes by Camden Lock.

Opening hours: London Zoo, all year round, 1000-1730 (admission charge).

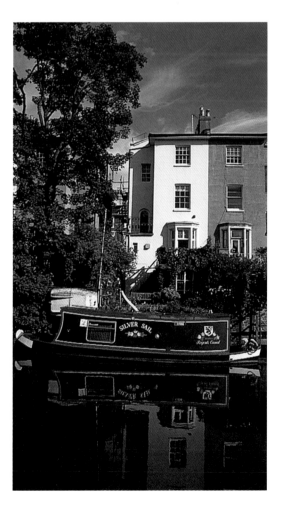

Regent's Canal.

pub) for a footbridge to the far side of the Regent's Canal. Walk back (eastwards) past the moored boats along the leafy towpath to Little Venice, where elegant, tree-lined Georgian properties look down on a triangular basin of colourful narrowboats.

It is not surprising to learn that the Victorian poet Robert Browning once lived nearby (the small island of weeping willows and nesting ducks that you can see is named after him); even today there is a studio and gallery moored here. By the bridge is the old Toll House, now offices for British Waterways, and beyond is the Waterside Cafe, an irresistible floating cafe and information centre (open daily in the summer).

Cross over the blue-painted bridge above the cafe, and as the Paddington arm of the Grand Union Canal disappears on the far side, carry straight on with the Regent's Canal, taking to the pavement above colourful towpath gardens (private) towards the 250 m-long Maida Hill tunnel. Spoil from its excavation was laid on landowner Thomas Lord's fields nearby - later to become Lord's Cricket Ground. Cross Edgware Road by the zebra crossing and go down Aberdeen Place; where this turns left by a finely-decorated Victorian pub called Crocker's Folly, take the alleyway opposite and return down steps to the towpath.

Opened in 1820, the Regent's Canal was built to link the Grand Union (or Junction) Canal with London's Dockland at Limehouse; but within 20 years of its construction London's first mainline station opened at Euston and the canal's commercial future was doomed. In fact you soon pass beneath the railway into Marylebone, but then after another road bridge the surroundings suddenly switch from urban to rural, and a deep wooded cutting takes you from modern flats to elegant period villas with terraced lawns stretching down to the waterside. This is the edge of Regent's Park, which you reach by leaving the towpath at the first footbridge (Charlbert Bridge). Once on the far bank, cross the Outer Circle.

Flower beds, Regent's Park.

Regent's Park (or *The* Regent's Park, as it's officially known) was laid out by architect John Nash between 1812-27 on Henry VIII's former hunting ground of Marylebone Park. Nash envisaged a series of 56 villas amid carefully landscaped grounds, plus of course a residence for his patron the Prince Regent (the Inner

Circle was intended to surround it). In the end only eight villas were built, and a public park resulted, but the carefully-designed gardens and lakes, together with the handsome Regency terraces that surround its southern half, continue to give the park a most civilised air.

Entering the park, take the right fork through gardens, then right again when the grassy open spaces appear. At the end of the Boating Lake go across two blue footbridges (note the distinctive sight of the London Central Mosque ahead) and turn left, around the far shore. Go back over the water via the handsome wrought iron Clarence Bridge, and left via the bandstand to reach the Inner Circle opposite the Rose Garden Buffet.

Go clockwise around the Inner Circle until, opposite the back of the open-air theatre, turn left to cross the Long Water, with its resident collection of waterfowl - as many as 45 types of duck have been recorded in the park. Turn right, and when the black railings end go across the grass towards the mock-Tudor Tea House.

Ahead is the Broad Walk, a wide tree-lined avenue that Nash intended to be the main drive of the park. Turn left on to it, and just past a rather weather-beaten fountain (erected by the long-defunct Metropolitan Drinking Fountain and Cattle Trough Association), turn left for a path through the shrubbery which skirts the south-western perimeter fence of London Zoo. Across it you may see dromedaries, vultures and even elephants!

At the Outer Circle, turn right for the main entrance to the zoo; otherwise cross over this road, the canal and Prince Albert Road onto Primrose Hill itself. Take the path up the left-hand side, branching off right to the summit, from where there are wonderful views across central London. The odd, angular construction made out of wire netting in the foreground is London Zoo's distinctive aviary, designed by Lord Snowdon.

View from Primrose Hill.

Drop down to the far left-hand corner, then re-cross the road using the pedestrian lights. Turn left, and after 150 m rejoin the towpath by Water Meeting Bridge, turning left underneath it, opposite a striking floating Chinese restaurant. The towpath becomes built-up once more, and leads all the way into Camden. A plaque on a warehouse wall explains that ramps were built into the canal along here to rescue horses that had fallen in after bolting at the sound of trains on the overhead bridge!

Camden, especially at a weekend, is a noisy, colourful, vibrant place. The lockside markets sell everything under the sun, there are pubs and cafes galore, and you will soon realise whether or not you are up with current trends. For the tube station and High Street, turn right at the lock bridge.

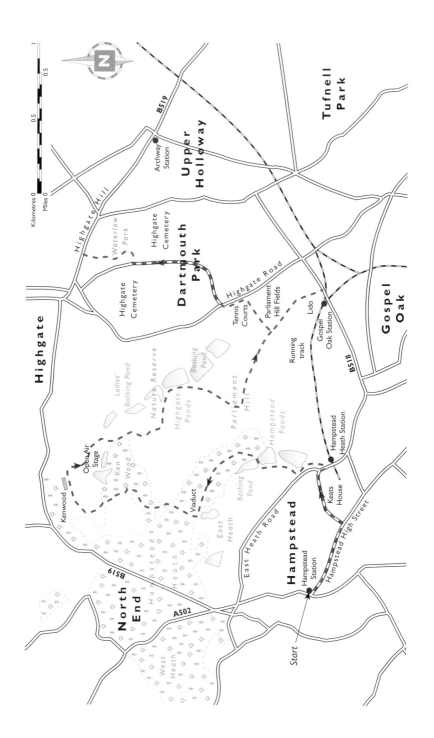

HAMPSTEAD HEATH AND HIGHGATE

Hampstead Heath is unique: 320 ha of woodland, heath, ponds and meadow little more than 6 km from Piccadilly Circus. London's best-known open space mixes sports pitches and outdoor bathing ponds with secluded nature reserves and unfrequented corners where you will hardly meet a soul. Not unnaturally, it is both a haven for wildlife and a means of escape for Londoners who can be found rambling, jogging, cycling, fishing, sunbathing, kite-flying, birdwatching, footballing, swimming, and other various and sometimes curious pursuits.

Begin at Hampstead tube station (the deepest on the network, 63 m below ground level). Walk down the cafe-lined High Street and turn left into Downshire Hill, then right into Keats Grove. Here you will find the Heath Library, and next to it Keats' House, where the poet John Keats wrote *Ode to a Nightingale* after hearing one singing in the garden.

Keats' House.

At the end cross East Heath Road (where those starting at Hampstead Heath railway station will join) and walk up the wide, tree-lined avenue on to the Heath, veering away from the car park, above a string of small ponds. A wide path crosses between the second (model boats) and the third (mixed bathing), and at the junction on the far side take the second

INFORMATION

Distance: 7.5 km (4.75 miles).

Start: Hampstead tube station or Hampstead Heath railway station.

Finish: Highgate.

Terrain: easy surfaced tracks and rough heathland/ woodland paths (slippery when wet). Moderately accessible for pushchairs/ wheelchairs, but heavy going after wet weather.

Public transport: Hampstead tube station (Northern line) or Hampstead Heath railway station (North London Line); buses 24, 46, 168, 268. From Highgate, buses 143, 210, 214, 271; or Archway tube station (Northern line) is an 800 m walk down Highgate Hill.

Refreshments: Many cafes and pubs in Hampstead and Highgate, plus tearooms at Kenwood House and Parliament Hill Fields.

For opening hours see page 76.

Opening hours:
Keats' House, daily
1000-1700; Kenwood
House, daily 1000-
1800 (1600 Oct-Mar);
Hampstead Heath
Information Centre,
Wed-Sun 1000-1700
(Mar-Oct), 1100-1600
(Nov-Feb); Highgate
East Cemetery, daily
1000-1700 (Apr-Oct),
1000-1600 (Nov-Mar)
(admission charge).

**Further
information:**
Hampstead Heath
Information Centre,
Parliament Hill Lido,
tel 0171 482 7073.

path on the left, uphill past a huge, branchless tree trunk. At the top, turn left on to a surfaced track and follow this for 500 m until you reach a viaduct above a pond that is usually covered with lily pads in summer.

Curiously isolated, the viaduct was built in the mid 19th century as part of an ill-fated project for a new road and houses. The battle to develop the Heath was epitomised by Lord of the Manor, Sir Thomas Maryon Wilson, who for 40 years defied conservationists with plans to build villas and the ongoing extraction of gravel and sand. It only ceased when he died in 1869; two years later the Hampstead Heath Act was passed, securing its future as a public open space.

Cross the viaduct and turn right, over another bridge, then up a wooded path to a clearing. Go through the gate in the railings opposite, and fork left through dense holly trees. This is the Iveagh Bequest, part of the Kenwood estate, a hushed and peaceful place. Keep left at another fork, passing a plaque remembering the storm of 1987 which destroyed 54 mature trees in this wood alone; then go through a gate on the left and across a culvert and then a meadow, and finally through a gate to reach Kenwood House.

The Viaduct, Hampstead Heath.

This handsome neo-classical pile stands proudly above open parkland that slopes down to landscaped lakes and woodland. Elsewhere there are flower gardens and a restaurant, while inside an important collection of paintings is open to the public. Each year, Kenwood plays host to a series of open-air evening concerts on summer weekends, when some of the grounds may be temporarily closed. Enquire at the Information Centre for further details.

Continue along the wide terrace in front of the house as it swings back towards Ken Wood, switching to a surfaced path the other side of the fence as you begin to drop downhill. Branch off across grass (right) to go through a clear gap in the trees, and then at the far side of the long meadow go through another gap and turn left. The partly-hidden pond through railings on your left is a nature reserve. Follow the surfaced path to the right of the model boating pond until the next, Highgate Men's Bathing Pond, where you should take the long, straight path half-right that climbs towards the bare grassy top of Parliament Hill.

The hill's name may have come about after Cromwell's forces stationed cannon here during the Civil War; another explanation is that Guy Fawkes and his fellow conspirators planned to meet on its top to watch Parliament burn. A mecca for north London kite-fliers, there is a wonderful panorama from its modest 97 m across the West End and City, and on a clear day St Paul's Cathedral and the smaller dome of the Old Bailey are easily visible.

From the summit, continue down the main path and branch right, past the athletics track, to visit the Hampstead Heath Information Centre at the Lido. It has details on all aspects of the Heath, plus displays and a children's corner. After this, retrace your steps and turn right, past the tearoom, and leave the Heath via the tennis courts at Parliament Hill Fields.

Highgate from Hampstead Heath.

Cross Highgate Road by the zebra crossing and walk up Swains Lane to reach Highgate Cemetery, which is in two parts. Entrance to the West Cemetery is by guided tour only; while the sprawling, leafy East Cemetery is the final resting place of the novelist George Eliot, actor Sir Ralph Richardson and, of course, Karl Marx. (But do remember that the cemetery is still used and respect the privacy of mourners.)

Beyond the cemetery turn right, into Waterlow Park, and follow the main path as it snakes upwards and leftwards above the pond in the bowl below, and out on to Highgate Hill. To your left are the cafes of Highgate; down the hill to your right is Archway tube station.

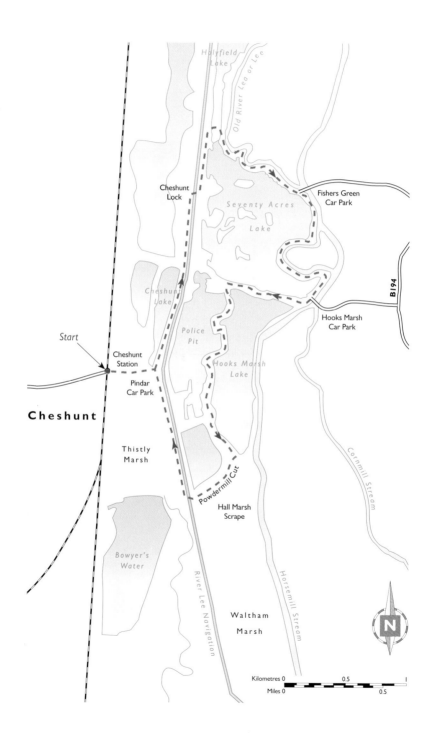

Holyfield Lake

Old River Lea or Lee

Cheshunt Lock

Seventy Acres Lake

Fishers Green Car Park

B194

Cheshunt Lake

Police Pit

Hooks Marsh Car Park

Start

Cheshunt Station

Pindar Car Park

Hooks Marsh Lake

Cheshunt

Thistly Marsh

Powdermill Cut

Hall Marsh Scrape

Cornmill Stream

Bowyer's Water

River Lee Navigation

Horsemill Stream

Waltham Marsh

N

Kilometres 0   0.5   1
Miles 0   0.5

LEE VALLEY PARK

Over the years the River Lee has been spelt in more than 20 different ways. The local authority seems to prefer 'Lee', but the long-distance footpath along its length is officially known as the 'Lea' Valley Walk. The Ordnance Survey is undecided, and gives both! The river's southern half is typified by a succession of lakes and reservoirs, centrepiece of which is the Lee Valley Park, Britain's first regional park, with a total water area greater than the Norfolk Broads.

The landscape and wildlife of the Park owes much to the hand of man. The lakes are the result of sand and gravel extraction, begun in the 1920s and since flooded. Although some pits were filled in, others regenerated naturally. They have provided a haven for wildlife, particularly birds; wildflowers have also benefited. Near Cheshunt Lock there is a large meadow of early and southern marsh orchids which have prospered in the ash-rich soil dumped here from local power stations.

From Cheshunt Station, turn right for Pindar car park at the end of Windmill Lane. Go through it and turn left on to the towpath of the River Lee Navigation, an artificial cut - you will meet the meandering 'Old River Lea' later on. The occasional swan waymark indicates that this is the route of the Lea Valley Walk, an 80 km trail from Bow in East London to Luton in Bedfordshire that has gained the London Walking Forum's seal of approval.

Follow it past Cheshunt Lake and under a bridge as far as Cheshunt Lock, crossing by the lock gate to connect with the circular walk (green arrows) around Seventy Acres Lake - turn left on to it for Fishers Green. (People with pushchairs or wheelchairs should cross the river by the bridge instead, going under it first, and turn left at the junction of paths on the far side.)

Follow the easy, gravel track around the edge of the lake, keeping right at a junction on the far side, past

INFORMATION

Distance: 5.5 km (3.5 miles).

Start and finish: Cheshunt Station or Pindar car park, Windmill Lane, Cheshunt.

Terrain: Flat, easy gravel tracks. Accessible for pushchairs/wheelchairs although the Lee towpath can get waterlogged in wet conditions, at which times the Park authorities recommend using the circular wheelchair walk which starts from Fishers Green car park. The different coloured waymarks you will see are for the Park's short circular walks (see noticeboards).

Public transport: Cheshunt Station (trains from Liverpool Street); buses 310, 311, 363 (Mon-Sat) - walk down Windmill Lane from centre of Cheshunt.

Refreshments: Three pubs near the station; occasional mobile snack bar at Fishers Green car park; but this is essentially a picnic walk, since there are tables and seats dotted all along the route.

Opening hours: Lee Valley Park Countryside Centre, Waltham Abbey (off A121), daily, 1000-1700 (summer), 1030-1600 (winter), closed Mon.

reed beds and swampy undergrowth, wooded islands and hidden pools. The array of birdlife can be appreciated immediately, but for an expert viewing position spend a few minutes inside one of the ten hides that have been specially constructed around the Park. One such is Waverley Hide, located just before the high green footbridge that leads to Fishers Green car park. (Hides

Footbridge at Fishers Green.

are open to the public on weekends and Bank Holidays, and to permit holders on weekdays.)

Inside the hide you will find identification charts, and notices of rare and interesting sightings. Remember to be quiet, and patient, and leave everything as you find it. As many as 200 different species of birds are seen in the Park each year, and in addition to the usual coot, moorhen, mute swan and Canada geese, you are likely to see great crested grebe, tufted duck, cormorant,

Near Bittern Hide.

yellow wagtail, reed warbler, heron, and perhaps the blue flash of a kingfisher. Winter visitors include goldeneye, smew, and the rare bittern.

Continue along the lakeside path. On your left the Old River Lea is lined with glorious willows, and in front are reedbeds where dragonflies and damselflies buzz among the bulrushes (or reedmace), river water crowfoot and the tall, reddish-pink flowers of purple loosestrife. Walk through Hooks Marsh car park following the sign for Cheshunt, and once over the raised metal footbridge, turn left on to a long, snaking path, signposted Hooks Marsh.

Go over a small wooden crossing at the end of Hooks Marsh Lake on to a gravel track, then turn sharply right for another, along Powdermill Cut. The name refers to the once important transport link to the former Royal Gunpowder Factory sited in the wooded area behind you, and still closed to the public.

On your right is an old wartime gun emplacement that has been preserved as a roost for bats; then further on is Plover Hide, where birdwatchers regularly focus their sights on Hall Marsh Scrape to spot both migrants and breeding birds, including little ringed

Waymarks.

plover and redshank. At the end of the Cut ignore the turning left and instead go ahead and right, over two small footbridges, which lead to a bridge back over the Lee Navigation at Waltham Common Lock. Turn right, and opposite the unshowy but neat brick lockkeeper's cottage, follow the towpath back to Pindar car park (watch out for the signpost to Cheshunt Station).

If you want to extend the walk, turn left at the end of Powdermill Cut to walk across Waltham Marsh, returning via the Lee towpath or the circular walk route along the shore of Bowyer's Water (see local noticeboard maps). Also, don't forget to fit in a visit to the Lee Valley Park Countryside Centre at nearby Waltham Abbey. It has displays and information on all aspects of the park, and you can visit the historic abbey, reputedly the burial site of King Harold.

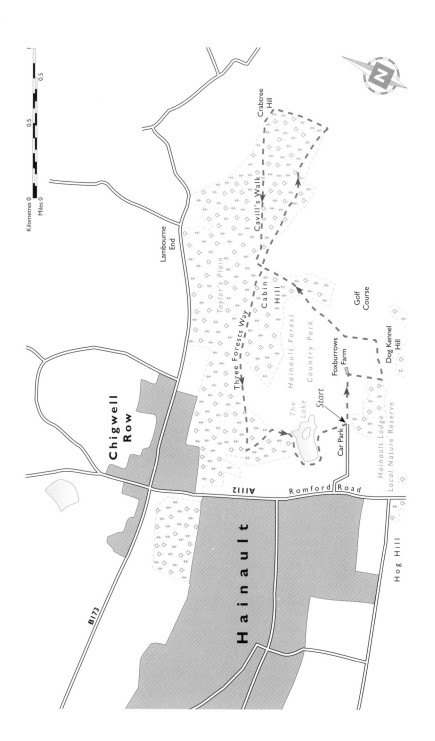

HAINAULT FOREST COUNTRY PARK

Now a rather isolated, tree-covered ridge, Hainault Forest Country Park was once part of the Great Forest of Essex that also included the wooded expanses of Epping and Waltham. Here, 150 years ago, charcoal burners built their huts and carefully burnt cut timber. The thick cover of oak, birch and hornbeam that they once worked now supports a healthy variety of woodland wildlife, and provides for a mostly quiet and certainly gentle walk.

Walk up the road past the cafe, and just before the park offices turn right on to a wide track between the animal enclosures up the flank of Dog Kennel Hill. Foxburrows Farm, established in the 1850s, is nowadays home to a collection of traditional and rare animal breeds. The wide, sloping field on your left, for instance, usually contains several Longhorn Highland cattle, resplendent in their thick shaggy coats and curved horns.

When you reach the top turn left, past some picnic tables by the fence. Keep the golf course on your right

INFORMATION

Distance: 6.5 km (4 miles).

Start and finish: Hainault Forest Country Park (main entrance), off Romford Road (A1112).

Terrain: Straightforward woodland tracks, muddy after wet weather when strong footwear is advisable.

Public transport: Buses 150, 247, 362 all stop on Romford Road, either outside or near the park entrance; or Hainault tube station (Central line), then bus 247 to Park entrance.

Refreshments: Cafe next to car park (open daily in summer; Fri-Sun over winter).

Opening hours: Park open daily from 0700, all year

Highland cattle on Foxburrows Farm.

- do not venture on to it at any time - and follow the clear track back down past former farm labourers' cottages and across the road where it continues opposite (ignore the parallel horse ride on the left).

After 800 m, and a very gradual ascent of Cabin Hill, the golf course on your right ends, and the path enters woodland. Turn right, just behind the display board and bench, and follow a track through the southern edge of the trees all the way to the corner of the woods.

The partly-visible golf course is soon replaced by ploughed fields, and this is a very peaceful and attractive place, with oak and silver birch lining the path. When you emerge from the woods, by another noticeboard, there is a track directly ahead that provides a link to Havering Country Park.

A little to the south is a place called Collier Row, once a collection of houses on the edge of the forest where charcoal burners lived (they were known at the time as colliers). Until the mid 19th century this was an important local industry, since charcoal was used in gunpowder, for iron smelting, and even in bakers' ovens. If you look closely in the forest today you can see the remnants of ponderous old hornbeam trees which the colliers used to regularly crop at about head height (an activity known as pollarding). By removing

Woodland fungi.

the main crown of the tree, its yield of wood was increased and its lifespan prolonged; it also prevented most of the young shoots being eaten by deer. Cutting took place before the limbs exceeded 10 cm (4 inches) in diameter, the maximum size used for charcoal burning, and also for firewood in London; this meant that hornbeam pollards were lopped every 18-25 years. It is interesting to note that woodland managers continue to experiment with this traditional technique, which has now been out of active use for nearly 100 years.

Turn left and follow the track uphill, between the edge of the wood and the field fence. At the top of Crabtree

Hill there are extensive views towards Havering and Harold Hill. Then follow the track into the forest once more, past a metal post marking the outer boundary of the former London County Council, and down past some isolated cottages. Beyond the last one, turn left on to Cavill's Walk which, as a notice explains, is named after wheelwright James Cavill, who lived at nearby Abridge during the last century.

The long, wide track through the ancient woodland is a delight: flowers and fungi are both in evidence, and woodland birds such as redpoll and hawfinch (fairly unusual for London) have been recorded here. Where the path merges with another, carry straight on, and then at a crossroads of tracks turn left to follow a broad ride back out of the woods - you were at this spot earlier! This time turn right for an open track, parallel to a horse ride, which runs long and straight through the middle of the forest. This is part of the route of the 96 km (60 miles) Three Forests Way, a circular long-distance path devised by the West Essex Group of the Ramblers' Association linking Epping, Hatfield and Hainault Forests.

Woodland ride, Hainault Forest.

Disregard all turnings until after 1.3 km you come to a small clearing, with patches of newly-laid gravel on the ground, and where your hitherto open track now enters some patchy woodland. Ignore this and go sharp left. Keep to the main track as it twists its way right and then left through trees to emerge by a lake; then follow it past the fishermen on the southern shore back to the car parks and cafe.

If you want to continue your exploration, cross Romford Road to Hog Hill and the Hainault Lodge Local Nature Reserve (main entrance off Forest Road). Formerly the site of a royal hunting lodge, the mainly oak and hornbeam woods now support a range of insects, birds and wild flowers.

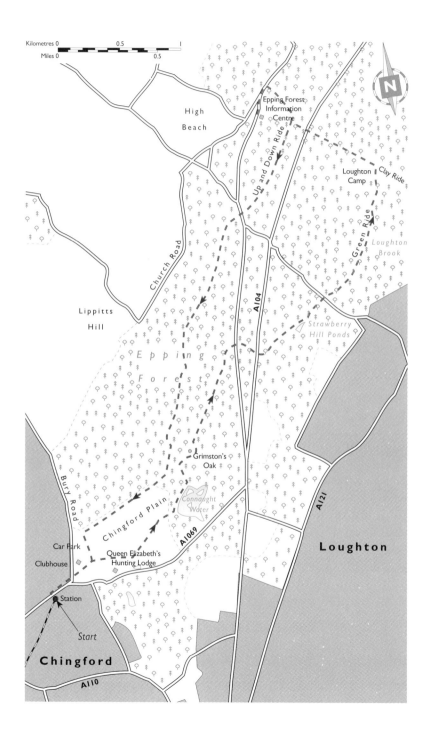

EPPING FOREST

INFORMATION

Distance: 11 km (7.5 miles).

Start and finish: Chingford Station (or car park on Bury Road, Chingford).

Terrain: Straightforward but occasionally rough woodland tracks. Strong footwear advisable.

Public transport: Chingford Station (trains from Liverpool Street); buses 97, 97A, 179 (Mon-Sat), 212, 313, 379, 444.

Refreshments: Tea hut and King's Oak pub by Epping Forest Information Centre; various outlets in Chingford.

Opening hours/further information: Epping Forest Information Centre, High Beach, Loughton, Essex IG40 4AF, tel 0181 508 0028, daily, 1100-1700 (closes 1500 Mon-Fri, Nov-Apr)

The Epping Forest Act of 1878 may not be particularly well-known today, but this crucial piece of legislation turned a royal hunting ground into a public forest, and ensured that nearly 2,400 ha of priceless ancient woodland would remain accessible to Londoners for generations to come. Today the Corporation of London, as the Forest's Conservators, still manage the woodland (mainly oak, hornbeam, birch and beech), ponds, heath and rough grassland that make up the 19 km-long Forest.

There are long-distance footpaths, such as the Centenary Way, Essex Way and the Three Forests Way (further details from the Information Centre); and numerous paths and forest rides. It is worth reminding walkers that these designated rides are also enjoyed by other users, and proper respect should be given to horseriders and cyclists should you wish to receive the same back.

From the railway or bus station in Chingford, turn right along Station Road to reach the heathy beginning of Epping Forest by the golf clubhouse (beyond this, off Bury Road, there is a large public car park for those arriving by car). Take the popular horse ride alongside the building, and soon branch half-right for another up past the back of Queen Elizabeth's Hunting Lodge, a splendid Tudor construction recently restored and open to the public. At the brow of the hill veer left, down to a junction of rides, and go straight over for a grassy path through bushes to Connaught Water.

Turn left and walk around the wooded edge of this beautiful if artificial lake, named after the Duke of Connaught, the first Ranger of the Forest. Wildfowl aplenty can be found here, especially the strikingly-coloured mandarin duck which nests in hollow trees around the lakeside. At the far left (north western) corner, opposite an island close to the bank, take a small path into the undergrowth, past a 'no cycling'

Connaught Water, Epping Forest.

sign, and in less than 200 m you meet a wide horse ride.

Turn right, go around Grimston's Oak, a fine old specimen apparently named after a cricketer, and continue straight on, keeping right at a junction. Continue over a surfaced lane then cross the busy A104. *Take the utmost care - this is a very fast road.*

On the far side, turn left out of the car park for the middle path into woodland (not the main surfaced ride nor the white-posted horse route) and before long you come to the first of the two Strawberry Hill Ponds. There are 150 ponds of varying sizes throughout the forest, which explains why Epping hosts large numbers of toads, all three species of British newt and nearly half of Britain's 42 species of dragonfly.

After the second pond, cross another road and continue down what is known as the Green Ride, with the deeply-eroded channels of Loughton Brook seen through trees on your right. The Green Ride was originally cut as a route for Queen Victoria, who officially opened the forest to the public in 1882, but unfortunately bad weather on opening day meant her ride was cancelled.

After 1.2 km of peaceful woodland, the ride climbs to
a clearing by two benches, where the so-called Clay
Ride enters from the right. Take the easily-missed
continuation of this (left) into the forest. Through the
trees on your left are the scanty remains of Loughton
Camp, an early Iron Age fort. Beyond the car park,
carefully cross the main road once more for a path
opposite, which soon joins another forest ride.

Grimston's Oak.

CORPORATION
OF LONDON

EPPING FOREST
CENTRE

Turn right and follow this all the way to the popular open space in front of the pub and tea hut, near High Beach. Once refreshed, make sure to go around the back and visit the excellent Epping Forest Information Centre. Outside there are views across the Lee Valley to Waltham Abbey and Enfield Chase.

Initially return the way you came, past the specially-constructed wheelchair walk, and along the aptly-named 'Up and Down Ride', but this time continuing for over 1 km until you reach a road crossing. (Do remember that, unlike other forest users, those on two feet have unrestricted access to the forest, and there is no reason why you should stick rigidly to horse rides if you want to explore the woods in more depth.)

The ride continues on the other side of the road. Stick to the main, direct route ahead of you, and at an S-bend where the trees thin out, ignore all tracks off. Back in the woods further on, go over another junction of paths; then at the next junction, go over the first crossroads and immediately take the next turning right.

You soon emerge on the edge of Chingford Plain. Keep to the track along the forest edge, taking care not to stray on to the rough grassland to your left if model aircraft are being flown (as they often are here). At the car park at the far end, turn left to return to Chingford.

Opposite: The Corporation of London now manage Epping Forest.

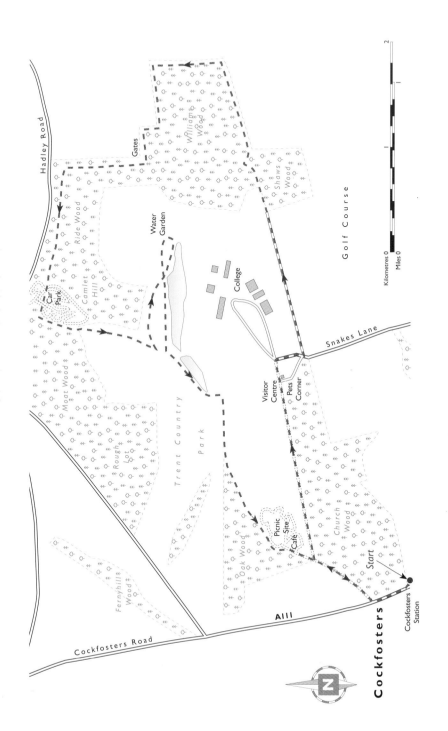

Hadley Road

Gates

Williams Wood

Shows Wood

Ride Wood

Camlet Hill

Water Garden

Car Park

College

Golf Course

Moat Wood

Rough Lot

Trent Country Park

Snakes Lane

Visitor Centre

Pets Corner

Oak Wood

Picnic Site

Café

Church Wood

Fernyhill Wood

A111

Start

Cockfosters Station

Cockfosters

Cockfosters Road

Kilometres 0

Miles 0

TRENT PARK

Trent Country Park is part of a former royal hunting domain still known as Enfield Chase, but today's fine park came about when George III presented 80 ha to his doctor, Sir Richard Jebb, after he had successfully treated the King's brother, who fell ill while on holiday in the Italian Tyrol at Trento - hence the park's new name. The grand house in the centre of the grounds was remodelled by a later owner, Sir Philip Sassoon, who entertained the likes of Lawrence of Arabia; during the Second World War it was used for the interrogation of captured German officers, including Rudolf Hess. Today it is part of Middlesex University, and although the house and its immediate grounds are private, the surrounding area, which includes extensive woodland, lakes, and lovely open parkland, provides a highly enjoyable day out with a range of attractions; in the first week of August the annual Enfield Steam and Country Show is staged here.

Turn right out of Cockfosters tube station into Cockfosters Road, and after 350 m turn right again through the park's main entrance. Go down the straight, traffic-free double avenue of limes into the heart of the estate. At the end is the Swiss Lodge

INFORMATION

Distance: 7.5 km (4.75 miles).

Start and finish: Cockfosters tube station or Cockfosters Road car park, Trent Park.

Terrain: Undulating park/woodland. Shaws Wood and Williams Wood can be very muddy in winter - boots or wellies needed.

Public transport: Cockfosters tube (Piccadilly line); buses 298, 299, 384.

Refreshments: Cafe by Cockfosters Road car park (open daily).

Opening hours: Park, daily, 0800-sunset, all year.

Vietnamese Pot-Bellied Pig, pets corner.

Visitor Centre, and behind is Pets Corner. As well as goats and sheep, there are rare breeds of pig.

The truly enormous Vietnamese Pot-Bellied is a sight to behold, and was a fashionable domestic pet in Britain in the late 1980s. The equally porky Middle White was popular between the Wars when, as a noticeboard explains, it was known as the 'London Porker'. Fully grown it weighs 240 kilos, or the equivalent of three men.

Continue to the end of the main drive with the campus in front of you and turn right, on to Snakes Lane, then left, for a long and straight concrete road on the college's southern perimeter. At the far end, go through a white gate and along a path into Shaws Wood. When you come to another gate, turn right, and very shortly left, to join a track around the eastern edge of Williams Wood. There are eye-catching views across farmland towards Enfield, with the high, wooded ridge of Epping Forest on the horizon.

Keep to the outer edge of the woodland and eventually swing around westwards, dropping down to meet a wider horse ride. Turn right and follow its twists and turns through the pines until it goes half-left between two facing gates. You can either go through the gate on your right for a clear footpath around the northern fringe of Ride Wood by Hadley Road; or stick to the horse-track as it canters along open ground in front of the woodland with views across fields.

The latter soon curves back into the trees, and where it is crossed by the previous footpath, turn left through a gate with a sign telling oncoming pedestrians to 'beware horses'. Proceed across two concrete-studded drives (they lead to a car park) and at a crossroads of tracks, turn left for the one signposted 'Lakes and Water Garden'. If you want to extend the ramble, go straight on for the woodland walk around Moat Wood and Rough Lot.

As you drop downhill and emerge into an area of rough meadow, turn left on to a path above the lake.

At the far end you can enjoy a circuit of the Water Garden, originally created by Sir Philip Sassoon, and after years of neglect restored in the early 1980s. In springtime there is a colourful display of shrubs and flowers amid the cool shade.

Walk back along the lakeside opposite the handsome old house that now serves as the main college building. Go over a path and past a second, smaller lake, lined with alder and willow and noisy with waterfowl; at the far end, turn left on

Trent Park.

to a rising track. This leads back up to the Visitor Centre, and also to a 1 km waymarked nature trail which visits woodland, pondside and a hay meadow. On the far side of the park, near the main entrance, there is also a 1.25 km trail for blind and visually impaired visitors, with tapping rails and Braille information boards.

However, if you are ready for a mug of tea and some mouth-watering apple pie at the cafe, don't go uphill now but turn right for the path along the bottom of the park and up through Oak Wood to the park entrance.

For a longer, linear walk in this area try the Pymmes Brook Trail, which has gained the London Walking Forum's seal of approval. It runs for 16 km from Monken Hadley Common via Trent Park and

Trent Park House.

Arnos Grove to Lee Valley Park; for more details see the notice-board in the car park or contact the Leisure Services Section at the London Borough of Barnet (two free leaflets are available).

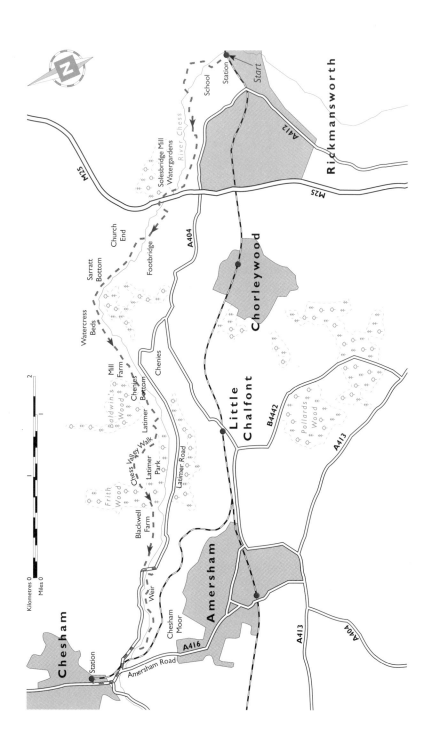

Chesham

Station

Amersham Road

Chesham Moor

A416

Amersham

A413

A404

Weir

Blackwell Farm

Chess Valley Walk

Latimer Park

Latimer Road

Frith Wood

Baldwin's Wood

Mill Farm

Chenies Bottom

Chenies

Little Chalfont

B4442

Pollards Wood

A413

Watercress Beds

Sarratt Bottom

Footbridge

Church End

A404

Chorleywood

Solesbridge Mill Watergardens

River Chess

M25

School

Station

Start

A412

Rickmansworth

M25

Kilometres 0   1   2
Miles 0   1

N

CHESS VALLEY WALK

This linear walk is rather longer than the others in this book, but it is hardly formidable! It takes you from London's leafy outer edge into the Chiltern Hills, offering easy gradients and - with the exception of the M25 crossing - generally peaceful and unspoilt countryside. The Chess Valley Walk was created by the Countryside Management Service in Hertfordshire, and Buckinghamshire County Council, both of whom efficiently waymark and maintain it. They produce a helpful leaflet guide (with map).

Leave Rickmansworth tube station and turn right, up Homestead Road, for the footbridge over the dual carriageway. Go across a field and down past an entrance to the Masonic School for Girls, built in the 1920s for the daughters of freemasons. You now follow a long, mostly hedged-in public footpath that squeezes between playing fields and then introduces you to the River Chess for the first time.

The Chess rises in the Chilterns and flows into the River Colne near Rickmansworth at Batchworth Lock (see Walk 23). Lack of public access prevents this being a truly waterside walk all the way, but where you are close to the clear, gurgling little river (as here) look out for dragonflies and kingfishers, and where willows weep down over hidden pools you may see moorhens and other waterfowl, and even the occasional trout.

Go across a road, and continue along a path between houses, keeping right at a fork; then over another road, and finally out into rough fields by paddocks. Skirt the outer fence of Solesbridge Mill Watergardens and walk along the foot of the motorway embankment to cross above the din of the M25.

After 200 m leave the road (right) for a public footpath to Sarrattmill. Approaching woodland, go through a gate and bear sharp left then right, following CVW waymarks. Soon you reach the riverside and swap banks via a delectable wooden footbridge.

INFORMATION

Distance: 16 km (10 miles).

Start: Rickmansworth tube station.

Finish: Chesham tube station.

Terrain: Easy field and woodland paths. Waymarked by Chess Valley Walk signs and blue discs showing a leaping fish.

Public transport: Rickmansworth and Chesham are both on the Metropolitan tube line. For bus times ring Buckinghamshire Traveline, 0345 382000; and Hertfordshire Traveline, 0345 244344.

Refreshments: Plenty in Rickmansworth and Chesham; occasionally available at Chenies Manor House Garden Room (house opening hours only) and Cakebread Cottage near Sarratt Bottom (summer weekends).

Opening hours: Chenies Manor House, Wed & Thurs, plus Bank Holidays, Apr-Oct, 1400-1700 (admission charge).

Further information: Rights of Way Section, Bucks County Council, County Hall, Aylesbury HP20 1UY (enclose SAE and mark envelope 'Chess Valley Walk').

Footbridge across the River Chess.

View from the footbridge.

Nearby, the willows and alder part to reveal an exquisite picnic spot on the grassy bank.

Follow a field edge path, cross a lane, then go down a drive and into another field. Ignore the footbridge and enter a thicket on a path (signposted Chenies) which becomes a metalled lane, and go ahead at a junction. On the corner is Cakebread Cottage, which on summer weekends often serves cream teas in its colourful front garden. When the lane bends right, go forward onto a track past watercress beds, once a common sight along the valley; then ahead on a clear path between fields usually full of grazing horses. After another stile, cross the north edge of Frogmore Meadows Nature Reserve, managed by the Herts and Middlesex Wildlife Trust, to reach Mill Farm.

To the left is a lane and then footpaths up to Chenies, a neat hilltop village visited mainly because of its semi-fortified Tudor manor house that hosted both Henry VIII and Elizabeth I in its time. The unspoilt interior includes period furniture and tapestries, and outside are well-tended sunken and Physic gardens (but check opening times in advance).

The shop at Mill Farm specialises in quality dairy ice cream, since the farm has a herd of pedigree Guernsey cattle. Continue through the farmyard and along a popular bridleway above the diminishing river, here almost choked by weeds. On the way you pass the so-called Liberty Tomb, where local brickmaker William Liberty was buried in 1777 at his own request. Apparently he was worried that, come the Resurrection, he would not be able to find all his own bones if buried with others in a graveyard.

Continue across the wide pasture and into the pretty village of Latimer, with its memorial to local men who served in the Boer War - and another, most curiously, to a horse which saved a man's life in 1900. Go left at the green for a waymarked path uphill towards Latimer House, a red brick pile built for the Cavendish family in 1863, and now a conference centre.

Turn right and follow the road for 700 m, finally leaving it (left) just past the entrance of Parkfield Latimer for a long field edge path. At the far left corner, descend a bumpy woodland ride to reveal terrific views across the valley. Go down a steep track and on through fields. Carry straight on where you join a surfaced lane, then almost immediately turn right for a short passage that leads to a gated field. Cross this to reach the main road.

Turn left and after 200 m turn right into Holloway Lane, until a public footpath to Chesham Moor branches off at the first corner. Despite the occasional vehicle and the presence of some very young fishermen, I still saw my only kingfisher of the Chess on this final stretch, so keep your eyes peeled!

When the track gives way to a field continue along its foot, until a right turning takes you through a gate past a fish farm and some factory units. Go over a metal bridge and turn left for a pleasant riverbank walk as far as a weir, after which it continues on the other bank. The area

Near Chenies.

known as 'the Moor' is actually an island, created in the tenth century by Lady Elgive, who built a mill here which was recorded in the Domesday Book.

Beyond Moor Road and the new sports centre go under the railway bridge and right at the roundabout, then into the centre of Chesham. The town's name was originally Caestlesham, meaning 'the water meadow by the pile of stones', the stones probably referring to the rock on which the parish church was built. The tube station is at the top of Station Road, on the right.

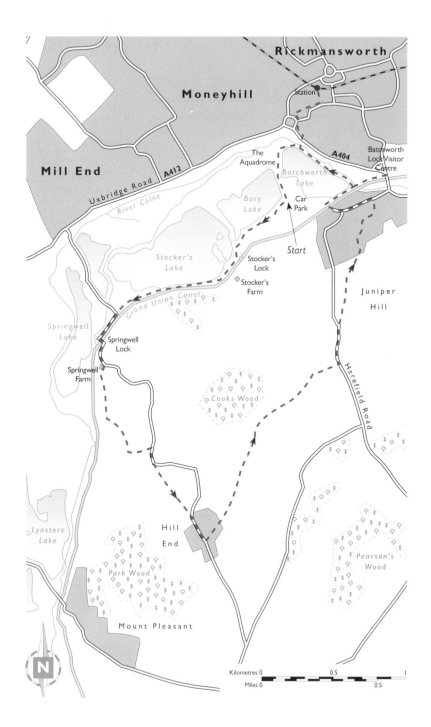

Rickmansworth

Moneyhill

Station

Mill End

The
Aquadrome

A404

Batchworth
Lock Visitor
Centre

*Batchworth
Lake*

Uxbridge Road   A412

River Colne

*Bury
Lake*

Car
Park

Start

*Stocker's
Lake*

Stocker's
Lock

Stocker's
Farm

Juniper

Hill

Grand Union Canal

*Springwell
Lake*

Springwell
Lock

Springwell
Farm

Cooks Wood

Harefield Road

*Lynsters
Lake*

Hill

End

*Pearson's
Wood*

Park Wood

Mount Pleasant

Kilometres 0   0.5   1
Miles 0   0.5

N

COLNE VALLEY

Colne Valley Park, which was established in 1965, is a narrow corridor of waterways and lakes along the edge of west London's urban doorstep. In the south is the Colne Valley Way, a 16 km waymarked path between Staines and Cowley, and at the other end - where you will be walking - is the new Colne Valley Trail which links Rickmansworth and Uxbridge (leaflet guides to both are available from the Visitor Centre near Denham).

An aquadrome, in case you aren't quite sure, is simply a place where lots of people gather to do sporty things on and sometimes in water. The one at Rickmansworth was developed from former gravel pits, now ringed by trees and pathways, and is very popular. You can watch all the activity as you leave the refreshment kiosk to walk along the southern bank of

Rickmansworth Aquadrome.

Stocker's Lock, Grand Union Canal.

INFORMATION

Distance: 7.5 km (4.75 miles).

Start and finish: Aquadrome car park, Frogmoor Lane (off Harefield Road), Rickmansworth.

Terrain: easy waterside tracks, but bumpy field paths may need fairly strong footwear. Some of the walk follows waymarks for the Hillingdon Trail.

Public transport: Rickmansworth station (Metropolitan line tube) is a 1 km walk - go down Station Road then right, along the High Street, and left at the roundabout for Riverside Drive and the start of the Colne Valley Trail through the Aquadrome; for bus details call Hertfordshire Traveline on 0345 244344.

Refreshments: seasonal kiosk by Bury Lake; Batchworth Brasserie by Batchworth Lock (Easter-Sept, weekends only).

Opening hours: Batchworth Lock Visitor Centre, Apr-Oct, Mon-Fri 1000-1500 (closed Wed), weekends 1100-1700.

Further information: Colne Valley Park Centre, Denham Country Park, Denham Court Drive, Denham UB9 5PG, tel 01895 832662.

Bury Lake, then on past the windsurfing club and canoe polo court. Go through a gate and turn left to reach the Grand Union Canal at Stocker's Lock.

Turning right on to the towpath, it is as if you have been transported back in time 150 years. Next to the neat lockkeeper's cottage is a classic, white-painted humped bridge, with horses grazing in the field beyond and a narrowboat or two lying idly by the bank. How peaceful it all is! Opened in 1805 as the Grand Junction Canal, the waterway engineered by William Jessop provided the Industrial Revolution with a key link between London and Birmingham - the M1 of its time.

Despite being extended and renamed the Grand Union in 1929, the canal struggled to compete with the railway and later the road boom, although it played an important role in moving war materials during World War II. Now leisure and not commercial traffic dominates; but instead of taking to the water, why not try out Britain's first National Waterway Walk, which stretches an impressive 234 km from Paddington, London, to Gas Street Basin in Birmingham.

Further on along the towpath Stocker's Lake, a nature reserve, may be glimpsed through trees on the right; on the far bank is a dilapidated building that was once a lime kiln.

At Springwell Lock, cross via the bridge and follow the lane as it climbs gently past cottages. This is the beginning of the 32 km Hillingdon Trail, a route that has gained the London Walking Forum's seal of approval, and which runs all the way across the borough to Cranford Park, near Hayes. You will be following its regular waymarks for the next 3 km, and look out for one now indicating a narrow footpath off to the right after 200 m where the lane bends left. The path becomes a wide, climbing track and there are fine views across the valley to the Chilterns.

Where the track ends, turn right on to a lane by stables, then in 120 m right again for a field path to Hill End. Halfway along the wide main street, turn left into a cul-de-sac signposted Hillingdon Trail Northern

Link - this is a spur from the main route that will connect with the London Outer Orbital Path (see Introduction). At the end cross a stile for a series of signposted paths with stiles across pasture, until eventually you climb a ploughed field and join a farm drive to reach Harefield Road.

View over Colne valley.

Turn left, and for 250 m follow the left-hand edge of the narrow road until a wide verge appears. *Take extreme care along this stretch.* Cross the road with caution, opposite the drive to Pipers Farm, for a signposted footpath into Juniper Dell and around the fringe of a new hilltop golf course.

After 400 m go left, over a stile, and descend between the sleepy semis of 'Ricky', turning right into Sherfield Avenue and then left, on to another public footpath which emerges opposite the supermarket. Turn left for Frogmoor Lane, and once over the canal bridge turn right for a towpath walk to Batchworth Lock Visitor Centre. You can meet *Roger*, one of the last wooden narrowboats to work the Grand Union and currently under reconstruction, or simply relax at the mouth-watering Batchworth Brasserie, situated above the lock gates. A canal festival is held here each year around May.

Retrace your steps along the towpath until opposite Tesco - there are moorings for waterborne shoppers - and go through a gateway to follow an easy path around Batchworth Lake back to the Aquadrome car park. Although popular with the likes of sailboarders and water-skiers, the lakes are also home to an array of wildlife, and there is a nature trail connecting Bury and Batchworth Lakes via the River Colne. Depending on the season, dragonflies and damselflies are often to be found near the water; while feeding grebes, tufted duck and coots are watched with envy by anglers huddled silently on the shore. They're probably still sitting there now.

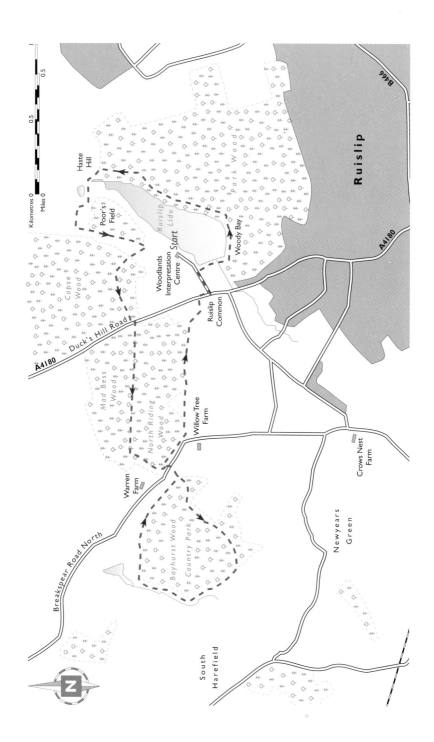

RUISLIP WOODS

Alido is defined as an open-air swimming pool or public beach, but here the large artificial lake nestling among Ruislip Woods in West London is the domain of water skiers and Canada geese, and swimming is strictly prohibited. Nevertheless, it is surrounded by attractive woodland which contains a healthy spread of accessible paths, plus an unexpected encounter with a narrow-gauge railway offering pleasure rides through the woods.

Beside the Waters Edge pub is the recently-opened Woodlands Interpretation Centre, with seasonal displays and interesting information on the arboreal stroll ahead. Begin by going around the southern shore of the lido to the 'Beach Cafe'. This is not so preposterous as it may sound, since there is indeed a wide area of sand which is popular on a sunny summer's

Ruislip Lido.

day. Of course both beach and lido are man-made, the latter created in 1811 with the drowning of the village of Park Hearn to feed the Grand Union Canal. Its more modern claim to fame is that some of Cliff Richard's classic 1960s film *The Young Ones* was shot here.

Beyond the beach is Woody Bay, the terminus of the Ruislip Lido Railway. This is a privately-managed line where miniature diesels pull open coaches through the woods to the end of the lido and back. You could even get a single ticket to Haste Hill and resume walking there!

INFORMATION

Distance: 8.5 km (5.25 miles).

Start and finish: Car park/bus stop at end of Reservoir Road, Ruislip Lido (off A4180).

Terrain: Flat woodland tracks, slippery and occasionally muddy if wet, when strong footwear will be needed. Some of the walk follows waymarks for the Hillingdon Trail.

Public transport: Buses 114, H13 (Mon-Sat); 331 from Duck's Hill Road (300 m walk).

Refreshments: Waters Edge pub; Six Bells pub, Duck's Hill Road.

Opening hours: Ruislip Lido Railway, every Sunday during the year, Saturdays (Apr-Oct), daily during school holidays; Woodlands Interpretation Centre, weekends and some weekdays in summer (call the London Borough of Hillingdon for further details on 01895 250647).

Ruislip Lido Railway.

Go through the barrier to the right of Woody Bay Station and turn left for a wide track through Park Wood, alongside the railway, until after 1 km both curve left around the end of the lido. The track continues past the platform at Haste Hill and after a junction bends sharply right. Here go through a narrow gap in the fence on your left, and emerging into the open, turn right on to a rough path along the edge of open ground known as Poor's Field, common land first recorded in 1295. It is now a carefully-managed Site of Special Scientific Interest containing orchids and harebell, a slender plant with bell-shaped blue flowers.

Path through Copse Wood.

After 50 m fork left, and go over towards the woods on the far side, but instead of entering them turn left on to a much wider track that runs parallel with the trees. As the ground rises there are views back over Poor's Field, and even a seat from which to enjoy them. After 500 m turn right, following signs for the Hillingdon Trail through Copse Wood (for further details of this route see Walk 23).

With four main component parts, Ruislip Woods altogether cover 291 ha, and contain around one tenth of Greater London's remaining semi-natural ancient woodland. Hornbeam can be found throughout the woods, used for centuries for coppicing to produce short poles and pea sticks; its ability to withstand regular cutting has also made it a widely popular tree with hedge-layers.

You will also see plenty of another fine English tree, the common or pedunculate oak, also used in woodland crafts; and its close relative the sessile oak, which can be distinguished from the common oak by virtue of the fact that its acorns have virtually no stalk. Also look out for sweet chestnut, aspen and the wild service tree. The age and quality of Ruislip timber is such that it was used in the construction of both the Tower of London and Windsor Castle.

The quiet, waymarked track through Copse Wood bears left to reach Duck's Hill Road. Cross carefully and continue along a more direct route through Mad Bess Wood, with reassuring signs for the Hillingdon Trail all the way to the western edge; then go over Breakspear Road North into Bayhurst Wood Country Park.

Ignore the Hillingdon Trail now, and follow the main, circular track around the outer edge of Bayhurst Wood, with lovely views towards South Harefield. There are picnic and barbecue sites, including one on the higher ground in the middle of the wood (in Old English, Bayhurst means 'wood on the hill'). About you a range of woodland birds can be seen. In the space of just five minutes I saw a lesser-spotted woodpecker and also the inconspicuous treecreeper, scuttling up and down a tree trunk in search of grubs and insects.

Return across the road and turn right for a path along the southern edge of North Riding Wood. Within 250 m this bends left, and you must turn off right for a short path that emerges at the entrance of a farm drive. Walk down the drive, and at the gate go over a stile on your right for an indistinct field-edge path by the fence. After 250 m go over a metal stile, back into the trees, and join a path (right) along the fringe of the woods eastwards.

Stick to the principal track as it wanders out of the main body of woods, forks right, and crosses two stiles before emerging by the Six Bells pub. Turn right and cross the road for Reservoir Road and the lido.

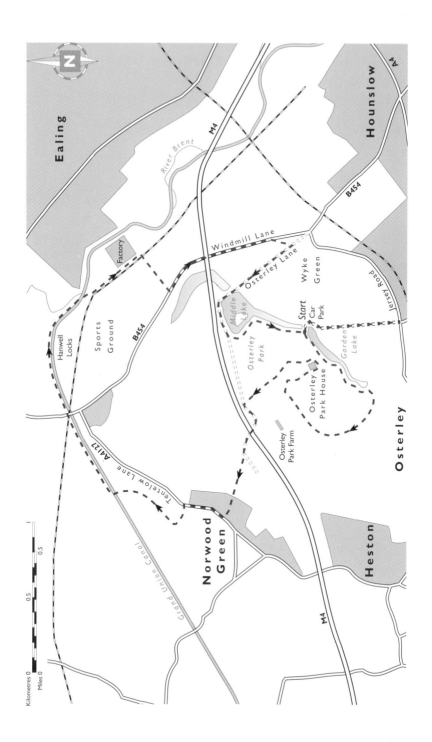

OSTERLEY PARK

There are a number of fine period houses in south-west London, such as Ham House, Syon House and Marble Hill, but for the best preserved country estate in Greater London visit Osterley Park. The house was built in 1575 for Sir Thomas Gresham, founder of the Royal Exchange, then 200 years later it was transformed into a neo-classical villa by the architect Robert Adam.

Osterley Park House, seen from the grounds.

INFORMATION

Distance: 9 km (5.5 miles).

Start and finish: Osterley Park House (National Trust car park), off A4.

Terrain: Easy paths and pavements. No special footwear necessary, unless wet. Park grounds (only) accessible for pushchairs/ wheelchairs.

Public transport: Osterley tube station (Piccadilly line) is a 1 km walk - turn left along the Great West Road, and left again into Thornbury Road; buses H28 and H91 (Mon-Sat).

Refreshments: Stables Tea Room (NT), Osterley Park House; The Plough Inn, Norwood Green and Hare and Hounds, Wyke Green.

Opening hours: Osterley Park House, daily, 30 Mar-31 Oct, Wed-Sun 1300-1700 (admission charge, NT members free). Park open all year, free.

His painstaking work, including plasterwork ceilings, furniture and even a landscaped park complete with lakes and mock temples, is carefully preserved by the National Trust. The extensive grounds alone, rich in mature oaks from around the world, are worthy of a whole day's exploration, but this walk combines a tour of the park with an excursion to the Grand Union Canal, and some very different scenery.

From the car park take the path around Garden Lake, with its floating Chinese pavilion. Between you and Osterley Park House is a lawn of elegant, mature Lebanon cedars. The large mound on the lakeside was once the Ice House, and was where ice removed from the lake in winter was kept for use in preserving foods the following summer. When the lake ends, take the left fork and follow the track around the wooded edge of the estate.

There are occasional glimpses of the house across the Great Meadow on your right, and nearing it once more you pass a small Doric garden temple, once used for picnics. Beyond this are the flower beds of the Pleasure Grounds, which you can walk though now by branching right (or keep straight on for the extra loop through the arboretum and pinetum). The National Trust is currently restoring the gardens and pathways to their original design.

Walk around either side of the four-turreted House, and providing you can resist the lure of the tearooms at this early stage, pass to the right of the handsome Tudor stable block in which they are housed and take the lane half-left; at the end of this go between the lodges and turn left again, out of the estate.

The lane crosses the ever-busy M4; when it bends left go down concrete steps to the right for a track through the middle of a cropped field. This becomes an alleyway between houses, crosses the end of a cul-de-sac, and emerges by The Plough Inn on Tentelow Lane, where you should turn right.

After 350 m turn left into Minterne Avenue, then first right into Melbury Avenue, and when this reaches the canal cross the bridge and turn left in order to double back on yourself under the bridge for the towpath

Lockkeeper's house, Grand Union Canal.

eastwards. This is the Grand Union Canal, and along the next 1.5 km you will pass tidy lockkeeper's houses, a straggle of patient fishermen, and if you're lucky some glimpses of local wildlife - on one of my visits, a canoeist enthused to me about a kingfisher he'd just seen. At one point there is a unique intersection where the canal crosses a railway (the old Southall-Brentford Docks line) and at the same time is crossed by a road bridge (A4127).

Before long you come to the six Hanwell Locks, the longest flight in London, lifting the canal 16 m in a length of 500 m. It takes a boat as much as an hour and a half to clear all the locks. The high brick wall on your left hides Ealing Hospital, and halfway along the lock sequence there is a bricked-up archway where once boats delivered coal to what was then a psychiatric hospital. The lock here was known as Asylum Lock. This is also where you briefly meet the Brent River Park Walk, an 11 km waymarked route along the Brent River from Brentham Open Space near Hanger Lane tube station to Brentford High Street (further details from the London Borough of Ealing).

At the sixth and final lock, cross carefully by the lock gate and follow the path up and around the left-hand edge of an old hay meadow to join a firm track alongside the railway. Don't cross here yet, but keep going for another 400 m and use the foot crossing at the corner of the industrial estate. Remember to stop, look and listen before crossing the line.

At the far side the path squeezes alongside the fence of a sports ground, and at the end turn left onto the pavement of Windmill Lane, which takes you back under the motorway. Opposite the Hare and Hounds pub, cross the road for a short path to the lodge at the end of Osterley Lane. Join this unmade road (a public bridleway) up to and around the northern end of Middle Lake, where an easily-missed kissing gate allows you to re-enter Osterley Park and follow the lakeside back to the House.

Osterley Park House.

INDEX

Opposite: Tower Bridge from Bermondsey.

Other titles in this series

25 Walks – In and Around Aberdeen
25 Walks – In and Around Belfast
25 Walks – The Chilterns
25 Walks – The Cotswolds
25 Walks – Deeside
25 Walks – Dumfries and Galloway
25 Walks – Edinburgh and Lothian
25 Walks – Fife
25 Walks – In and Around Glasgow
25 Walks – Highland Perthshire
25 Walks – The Scottish Borders
25 Walks – The Trossachs
25 Walks – The Western Isles
25 Walks – The Yorkshire Dales

Other titles in preparation

25 Walks – Cowall, Arochar and Bute
25 Walks – Down
25 Walks – Fermanagh
25 Walks – Skye and Kintail

Long distance guides published by The Stationery Office

The West Highland Way – Official Guide
The Southern Upland Way – Official Guide

The Stationery
Office

Published by The Stationery Office and available from:

The Stationery Office Bookshops
71 Lothian Road, Edinburgh EH3 9AZ
(counter service only)
South Gyle Crescent, Edinburgh EH12 9EB
(mail, fax and telephone orders only)
0131-479 3141 Fax 0131-479 3142
49 High Holborn, London WC1V 6HB
(counter service and fax orders only)
Fax 0171-831 1326
68-69 Bull Street, Birmingham B4 6AD
0121-236 9696 Fax 0121-236 9699
33 Wine Street, Bristol BS1 2BQ
0117-926 4306 Fax 0117-929 4515
9-21 Princess Street, Manchester M60 8AS
0161-834 7201 Fax 0161-833 0634
16 Arthur Street, Belfast BT1 4GD
01232 238451 Fax 01232 235401
The Stationery Office Oriel Bookshop
The Friary, Cardiff CF1 4AA
01222 395548 Fax 01222 384347

The Stationery Office publications are also available from:

The Publications Centre
(mail, telephone and fax orders only)
PO Box 276, London SW8 5DT
General enquiries 0171-873 0011
Telephone orders 0171-873 9090
Fax orders 0171-873 8200

Accredited Agents
(see Yellow Pages)

and through good booksellers

Printed in Scotland for The Stationery Office by c.c. No 70343 50c 4/97